Insider Threat Prevention

By

Raymond Leslie Newkirk,
Psy.D., Ph.D.

Printed in the United States of America

Systems Management Institute, Orlando, Florida 32835.

This book is available at a special discount when ordered in bulk quantities. For more information, contact Publications Sales Department, SMI Press, Orlando, Florida 32835, Tel: (407) 864 7756

www.drraynewkirk.com

www.smirsp.com

Table of Contents

The better the Insider Threat Prevention, The better the Insider Threat Mitigation. Solid ITP = Solid ITM

Acknowledgements

This work emerged from a lifetime of experience assisting organizations, teams, and individuals with finding inventive ways to solve problems more rapidly. As you move from country to country and culture to culture in search of inventive solutions to problems that are more common than one would ever imagine, you begin to notice several patterns emerge that reduce some of the mystery that shrouds the nature and character of human relationships including: How we form them; how we manage them; how we end them, and how we overcome them?

This is the stuff of life. Life is relationship living. In Christianity, we believe in God as Relationship. — Raymond L. Newkirk

If you ask how I describe human life, I would answer you this way: Life is Relationship. For good or bad, from hope to hopelessness, from self-doubt to confidence, from Ego to Self-Esteem, and from life to death, I would tell you that human life is formed, nourished, developed, enjoyed, and even made miserable through relationship, from birth to death. From the day you meet your mother to the day you meet your Undertaker you pass through life in relationship. How you

manage your relationships says everything about how you will become a fully human person imbued with the capacity for living a life of unique significance. We are creatures with the capacity to reason well, true; but human life is considerably more emotional than rational. Rationality is a power we possess to navigate life on a material planet. However, we feel more than we think. We use reason occasionally to assist in decision-making, but use our emotions most often to navigate the core experiences of our lives.

Think about this: Reason concerns the rules of logic, but emotion flows from the values we hold dear. Emotions represent value judgments, and reason represents logical conclusions, the if-then-else side of life. The decisions we make based on the value judgements we render often conflict with the decisions we conclude from deduction or induction. This is how we live human life on planet earth. Other places, I am not so sure.

All my life, Wise people have told me that the power of reason makes us human. We are the "rational animal". I guess, then, some people are more human than others. Does this make the artist less human than the scientist? Or, are we speaking about the human potential for rational thought so that the scientist is actually a human being and the artist is potentially a human being?

Moreover, the claim that human beings are "rational animals" is rather simplistic because human beings are more than animals, as Aristotle suggested. Although we do have the powers that animals share such as reproduction, self-mobility, growth, and so forth, we enjoy powers beyond those of brute animals like spiritual development, cultivation of virtue, and creative powers of the imagination.

An animal has body, like a rock has material volume occupying space, but an animal is not a rock. A rock requires transitive motion through an external agent to move it, while an animal enjoys imminent motion from within to move itself. So an animal enjoys the powers of a rock in having existence and a body, but exceeds rocks with its own many powers not enjoyed by rocks. In like manner, human beings possess powers not enjoyed by animals.

Human beings are, in fact, beings governed by conscience and the Cardinal Virtues. While we do not call animals "self-moving rocks", we really ought not to call human beings "rational animals". We are considerably more than that.

The problem for human beings here is one of reconciling our emotional powers with our rational powers. It is more than a matter of being "rational animals or "emotional animals". Being more than rational animals who enjoy the power of emotional judgment, the question persists: What kind of creature are we if not a rational animal? What is the influence of virtue in all of this?

Throughout their lifetimes, human beings experience multiple environments concurrently. As self-directed evolutionary beings, we share many of these environments in common with people around the world. We also experience these environments uniquely in ways that reflect our personal interests, commitments, beliefs, and aspirations as social beings. The three environments that most impact the development of this book and Parts Two and Three that follow it are the:

- Via Virtutis, the Way of Virtue
- Via Inventiōnis, the Way of Invention, Creativity, or Problem Solving
- Via Rationis, the Way of Reason, Structured Thinking, or Logic

For Fely & Mary

About this Series

This book series spans four volumes. The first identifies the pieces to the Insider Threat Prevention Cyber Security puzzle, the ITPCS Puzzle. This, the Third Book in the Series, defines the environment for putting the pieces together. The third examines the strategies of the Insider Threat Prevention Cyber Security Unification Program. The fourth describes the Continuous Performance Management and Insider Threat Prevention Cyber Security Unification Framework. Although each book presents an independent look at a specific segment of the entire unification program, mastery of the Framework requires you to create a roadmap of the entire landscape of the Insider Threat Prevention Cyber Security-Enterprise Architecture.

This series differs from the more customary presentations on Insider Threat Prevention Cyber Security. Rather than drilling down into the usual technical presentations of Cyber Security, I have focused on a behavioral and psychological solution to the challenge of building a unified ITPCS-Enterprise Architecture. Naturally, this focus tremendously increased the volume of material that could be included in each book. So, I had to make some choices about the paths I had to select. These books reflect my decisions. As you will see, I highlighted the strategic vision rather than the operational. In this regard, I focused more on the possible strategies for unification rather than the number of workflows involved in technical Insider Threat Prevention Cyber Security.

Special Acknowledgements

These four environments, and the people that inform them, have contributed to building the world we live in today. Their efforts will contribute to the future even more than they do now as Artificial Intelligence begins to impact society in even more potent ways. So, let me ask you several important questions. Do you know enough about Artificial Intelligence to life or dislike it? Is intelligence, real and actual intelligence, ever artificial. Do you realize that "Artificial" Intelligence will radically change the lives of millions of people because a few people have strong opinions about how it can shape the future of humanity?

Why do I bring this up now as I am writing about Insider Threat Prevention Cyber Security? Obviously, you already know, don't you? Think about it as an ITP CS specialist. How will ITP evolve with the introduction of A/I nearly everywhere, especially in the workplace. I am already hearing echoes out there about A/I eliminating 50% of all the jobs in this country. Unfortunately, I do not hear much about what is going to replace all of these jobs. Sadly, I have met a few people who are so taken by A/I that they are indifferent to the social changes that will ultimately emerge through the world, not only here in the good ole USA. We are not moving into a boring future. Having said this, I would like to acknowledge some of people who have assisted us in our efforts to shape the future for the good of humanity.

First Order Cybernetics

- Mathematics: Ashby & Weiner
- Physiology: Shannon
- Information Theory: Weaver
- Computing: McCulloch
- Engineering: Prigogine
- Control Theory: Bateson
- Anthropology: Mead

Second Order Cybernetics

- Biology of Cognition: Pask
- Experimental Epistemology: Maturana
- Family Therapy: Bowen

The Systems Sciences

- Interdisciplinary Movements:
  - First-Order Cybernetics
    - Science Studies

The Systems Approaches

- Management Cybernetics: Beer, Espejo
- Critical Systems: Jackson & Flood
- Critical Systems Heuristics: Ulrich
- Systemic Inquiry: Checkland
- Applied Systems: Checkland
- Systems Failure: Applied Systems: Checkland
- Information Systems: Stowell, Wood-Harper
- Systems Agriculture: Spedding, Badwen
- Social Systems: Buckley, Vickers
- Management Science: Ackoff
- Soft OR: Management Sciences, Ackoff
- Systems Analysis: RAND Corp.
- Management Learning: Schon, Argyris
- Systems Dynamics: Forrester, Meadows, Senge
- Whole Earth SD: Macy
- Systemic Complexity: Capra
- General Systems Theory: Bertalanffy
- Second-Order Cybernetics: Von Foerster
- Operations Research: Beer, Churchman, Ackoff
- Complexity Science; Ashby

Dedication

Welcome to a newer, simpler, and more effective way of navigating the professional minefield you call work. I dedicate this book series to everyone who suffers from the assault of painful and ineffective colleagues. Whether you are a member of the Board of Directors or a new hire beginning your career, no one wants to work with colleagues who characteristically produce more turmoil than satisfaction and disaster than productivity.

I wrote this book for all of us who at some time or another had to snatch victory out of the jaws of defeat and overcome the "strangeness" of colleagues we could rarely understand. If you are a Millennial, this book is especially for you. If you cannot relate to such a situation, this book is really for you. I wrote this book for everyone who looks at their organization and murmurs: "This place really doesn't make any sense. I just don't get it."

Well guess what? A lot of people just don't get it, especially the ones who think they do. If you get it, answer me this: Are you the kind of person who should recruit other people to work with you? Are you good for others? Are you really a good person who should be invited onto a team responsible for producing critical deliverables? Simply put: Should people want you as a colleague? Will you be good for them, or only good for yourself? What do you think? Have you ever thought about it? If not, you probably already have your answer. Some people are not even good for themselves.

I wrote this book for all of us who are currently building our careers and for the generations who will follow in our footsteps. This book emerged to assist you with navigating the hidden influencers that energize the workplace. These are the sparks that make-or-break effective performance. These are the sparks that produce the painful or joyful lives we live. I tip my hat to all of us. Now let us get busy and achieve something great with our careers. Why settle for less?

"I t's Not Very Often You Get to See Into the Development of a Cyber Terrorist. Successful Insider Threat Prevention Requires This."

— Raymond L. Newkirk

Preface

Insider Threat Prevention Cyber Security (ITPCS) is scary. In the first place, ITPCS challenges the most knowledgeable people in the organization. In the second, ITPCS is disastrous when it fails. A single criminal incident can completely ruin a company and render the company completely out of business (OOB). As far as I can remember, we have always faced the challenge of Insider Threat Prevention. Cyber Security, however, is the complicating factor today.

Today, ITPCS has become a chronic problem for executives and the organizations they lead. You would probably be correct to guess that about forty percent of all Cyber Security incidents result from malicious insider attacks. Insider cyber-attacks are more expensive than the attacks of external hackers. While "credentialed" Insiders attacks leave the most damage behind, the malicious insider attacks perpetrated by malicious outsiders through coercion often cause the most damage.

Here is a perennial fact: Insider Threat Prevention is fundamentally behavioral and psychological. Highly secure technology assists ITPCS, but it is not enough. ITP begins with people, moves to process, and terminates with technology, always facilitated by people. ITP is a direct attack on an organization's information resources.

Anything can be a target such as data, Intellectual Property, Trade Secrets, and Knowledge Applications. Malicious success requires Cyber Terrorists to discover where the organization's targeted information resources are located as well as the rules governing access and usage. These rules enable teams to manage data classification, access governance, data sharing, monitoring, procedures and controls, legal and cultural considerations.

The missing key to stopping malicious insiders is, of course, not hiring them and selecting them out early during the customary probationary period. Since malicious insiders can operate more silently and inflict more damage than outsiders, designated managers have to pay attention to the "lateral movement" activities of their employees as they access the information systems internally and externally.

While everyone relies on technology to assist with ITP CS, the Cyber Terror threat still exists. SIEM, Data Loss Prevention, User Behavior Analytics, Privileged Access Management, and User Activity Monitoring all fall short and are defeated by smart criminals. There is no doubt that these approaches can be helpful in reducing the severity of attacks. However, they are often helpful only after the attacks have occurred. Nevertheless, they can help management reduce the success rate of future attacks by preempting, detecting, and responding to the lateral movements of trusted insiders.

Although this "Suppression Approach" has become customary when insiders reach beyond their credentials to capture or disrupt an information stream, an innovative insider can defeat it, especially if he or she is knowledgeable about the embedded exposures hidden in the targeted systems such as "temporary" connections and credentials that by default have become permanent.

These careless mistakes increase the pressure on organizations to employ an expanded range of Cyber Security practices such as the use of data deceptions that mimic targeted data and files. Additionally, Cyber Security specialists may employ systems that collect highly accurate forensic evidence that arm first responders to resolve exfiltration more rapidly.

Companies adopt Continuous Performance Management to build and maintain cultures of trust, collaboration, and cooperation. Although trust is important among teams, it has to be earned. Blind trust fails the test of reasoned action. Senior management of CPM-designed organizations, above and beyond most other organizations, must continuously enhance their organizations' Insider Threat Prevention Cyber Security defenses.

Executives expect CPM organizations to remain consistently vigilant about the threat of Cyber Terrorism. Managers expect their team leaders to protect their systems, networks, and people against the constantly emerging attack techniques perfected by the malicious Cyber Terrorists inside and outside the company.

Insider Threat Prevention Cyber Security teams succeed whenever they prioritize, investigate, and respond to malicious insider attacks well enough to both reduce the risk of insider threats and prevent the occurrence of every targeted attack, and I do mean "every".

Raymond L. Newkirk, Psy.D., Ph.D., Ph.D. Th.C.

Orlando, Florida

Christmas Eve, 2019

The Formative Questions

What Do You Deserve?

Your career can be a rewarding life-long experience. It can be an enduring and wonderful gift. Or, it can become a dismal punishment whenever you ignore Moral Wisdom. Career success, however, is a lot like the weather: Everyone talks about it, but no one does anything about it. Sound familiar? So what kind of career do you want?

If you choose to accept a miserable situation, you may be the cause of your misery.

Where Do You Fit In?

Developing effective skills in Cyber Sensitive Environments requires a combination of soft-skills, hard-skills and personal qualities unimagined only a decade ago. University did not prepare you for this, but Moral Wisdom does.

Do You Know These Few Relevant Terms?

Moral Wisdom; Continuous Performance Management; Cyber Security; Insider Threat Prevention; Archetypes; Workplace Relationships; Resilience; Excellence; Existential Hunger; Applied Intuitive Solutions™; Knowledge Base Systems; Mobility; Human Activity Systems; Evolutionary Guidance; Design Inquiry; Coaching; Trust; Zero Tolerance; Invincible Ignorance; Cardinal Virtues; Sociopathology; Problem-Based Learning; Case-Based Reasoning; Evidence-Based Solutions; Traces-Based Reasoning; Unified Problem Solving Method; Unified Problem Solving Method Description Language.

Agony, If Nothing Else, Is Life's Faithful Retribution for Entering an Ill-Advised Workplace Relationship — Raymond L. Newkirk

Introduction to the Series

I wrote this series to address the dramatic challenge of Insider Threat Prevention Cyber Security. This is a much-ignored urgency in this time of Cyber Terror. The work began as a single paper about the dangers of Insider Cyber Threats, but the incessant questions of colleagues led me to see the need for a more detailed and expansive evidence-based work that can guide workplace practice.

This series addresses The Psychology of Insider Threat Prevention in a practical sense by discussing the need to "Unify", not integrate, the CPM organization and Insider Threat Prevention discipline.

I chose Continuous Performance Management (CPM) as a model of discussion for two reasons. First CPM is an extremely popular Human Resource Management model for organization design. Secondly, CPM vastly increases the danger of an Insider-generated Cyber Attack that can rapidly destroy an entire enterprise, and few seem to note this. I chose the Problem of Workplace Psychology as the overarching theme to coherently tie the components of the "CPM-ITPCS Unification" Program together.

I have studied the problem of Insider Threat Prevention Cyber Security in the USA, Europe, Asia, the Middle East, Australia, and all points south for more than 50 years. In the beginning, no one called it Insider Threat Prevention Cyber Security. People used novel expressions I will not dare to repeat. When I speak of "prevention", I mean A Priori Prevention, prevention before a threat even requires mitigation. This is challenging.

Part One identifies the pieces to the puzzle, Part Two discusses what to do what all the pieces after you identify them, and Part Three presents a Unified Model of CPM and ITP Cyber Security. I use Behavioral Science and Psychology to clarify the depth of the problem and the range of the strategies available for delivering ITP CS.

I hope you find each Part stimulating. I write this series to remove the intellectual cobwebs that are so common today. Success with this Insider Threat Prevention Cyber Security requires curiosity, interest, dedication, abundant study, and practice.

Insider Threat Prevention Cyber Security emerges as a Human Activity System in which the components are human beings. You know what this means right? Human Beings are incredibly creative and unbelievably destructive. We have to be more creative and better enterprise designers. You will never have time to be bored.

Ray Newkirk
Orlando, FL
08-21-2025

1: Demise of Axiomatic Ethics

Introduction

Welcome to a new adventure in which Millennials, Cyber Terrorists, and Continuous Performance Managers (CPM) take center stage. As you race through these pages, you will find that this work transcends previous discussions about digital transformation in the workplace. As we proceed from one page to the next, please remember that while everyone has an opinion, not every opinion is an informed opinion. Perhaps this book can reduce this insufficiency. A critical mind, not a mind full of criticism, is the only prerequisite to this work.

Our journey through these pages spans an interesting selection of seemingly unrelated topics. You will enjoy quite a cognitive stew. We will begin with a few pounds of Existential Hunger adding a consideration of the kinds of relationships it forms. We next season with a pinch of Moral Wisdom, values, and virtues.

Finally, to reduce any bitterness, we add a measure of Insider Threat Prevention and Human Activity Systems, with a reduction of organization design, performance management, strategic innovation, and professional growth. This recipe will satisfy your hunger for potent solutions to your own problems. Finally, following dessert, your will generate a number of new questions without building ill-will among team members.

Everything discussed in this work will never directly criticize any person, place, or thing. Never say never, right? The author simply discusses situations and events in a way that first enables us to better understand the challenges we face. We then seek potent courses of action to rapidly resolve them. This work encourages you to reframe discussions about Continuous Performance Management and Cyber Security as a more far-ranging behavioral topic of sociopathology than commonly envisioned.

I encourage you to think deeper and more profoundly about the issues you believe you understand while connecting your hearts and minds more humanely to the design of a more appropriate problem-solving process. This kind of approach to problem-solving is the beginning of the process to become fully human because it breaks through the numerous pre-suppositions that many people hold dear about the workplace without proper reason.

When contemplated with an open mind, this book delivers a challenging, thoughtful, and entertaining experience. The work raises several inter-connected topics in a fresh way so that you can expand your mind, not blow your mind. This work will expand your vision of the workplace as it requires you to focus on the issues discussed using a systems perspective.

This work indirectly illuminates the career path ahead by presenting the opportunity to expand your vision-building capacities. However, you must energize your rational processes yourself. Mastering this book will enable you to escape the dulling world of everyday work life by reducing the emotional conflicts you experience while concurrently sharping your intellectual capacities. Life does not present such an opportunity every day, unless you read my books.

Reading this book offers a real gift if you are up to it. I designed this book to assist you with advancing along the path of becoming a potent human being as you build your career and manage your life.

> **Many people slide by you know. They do the dance; they weave in and out of situations; they attempt to charm life and become the smooth operators that people sing about in pop culture, and they deceive their followers and fans.**

You see these people every day. They already think they have it made, that they have the right education to get them ahead in life. However, heads do roll and people sooner or later have to confront themselves. Ultimately when the conditions are right, these people feel the unease of the question that everyone has already asked about themselves a thousand times a thousand: "How human am I really?" No matter what, everything eventually ends.

The Age of Fragmented Rationality

In this current age, a time I refer to as the "Age of Fragmented Rationality," many people enjoy their lives without a thought to how much wisdom has evaporated over th e last twenty to thirty years. A number of these people have little idea about how much they are missing out on the substance of the truly human adventure found in a full life. It is a terrible tragedy to be unaware of one's capacities and skills and potentialities.

It is likewise a terrible tragedy to be so consumed with so much stress for so long that the mind makes a wrong turn to get out of its own way. True, every age has its own advantages and disadvantages. Previous generations, however, valued more highly the things that made human life really human. This included things like morality, ethics, virtue, and oh yes, the discipline of really thinking well, that is, thinking well below the surface of the merely social conventions of dominant groups.

Today people merely assume that they are human beings simply because their mothers and fathers probably were. However, it takes work to become truly human. A person has a right to constrain one's own existence, of course. Nevertheless, a person makes a great mistake, whenever he or she attempts to constrain the existence of another. Is it not more comfortable when human beings encounter other human beings along the journey called life?

I designed this work to assist you with reducing the unnecessary complexity of your professional lives. This work does this in several ways. First, the work assists you with the recovery of the kind of lost social knowledge that makes human life more potent. Second, the work enables you to master an innovative point-of-view about professional life without starting World War III. Third, the work delivers the Moral Wisdom that enables you to change the direction of your life if you so desire.

Here, you can pause for a minute, take a break, and think about yourself and your colleagues in a newer, freer, and certainly more potent way. You can learn more realistically how to connect your heart with your mind or your mind with your heart, healing the "substantial fragmentation" that is the reality of people today. Fourth, the work delivers the Moral Wisdom, skills, and expertise that enables you to gain better control over your professional life. Here, you learn to effectively navigate the one or two colleagues who bother you the most.

Cultivating the Process Models

This work delivers a Moral Wisdom Process Model that enables you to cultivate and maintain potent professional relationships. Moreover, it enables you to navigate the dreaded social situations that impede your career. In sum, this work assist you with forming the relationships you should form, avoiding the relationships you should avoid, and exiting the relationships you should exit. Professional success in the Digital Age requires the in-depth Moral Wisdom that enables you to navigate sociopaths at work.

Welcome to the Third Dimension of my Human Relationship Process Model. Here we concern ourselves with the influence of intrinsic and instrumental values on the formation of potent relationships and the clusters that these two kinds of values form: social responsibility, mastery, self-development, relationship, continuity, and lifestyle. Here we see that some values become essence-specific and others become aligned values.

"Lived" values become so much a part of us that we forget that we have them. These are habitual. If the habitual values compel a high order of behavior such as truth, love, respect, we call them virtues. If they compel low order behavior such as dishonesty, theft, manipulation, meanness, we call them vices. We can characterize relationships by the values that compel and guide their actions. One ought to think about how values influence the nature of relationships as we begin to think about the character of the relationships we form.

Simple Joy of a Values Inspired Relationship

Regardless of the relentless advance of scientific progress, life today is often more complex than at any time in history. Even indirectly, global situations impact the lives of every American corporation. No one escapes the march of history, from the household to the workplace. Compared to the stress people experienced in the 1970's and 1980's, more people have become overwhelmed by the stresses of life today.

For example, modern conveniences such as 24X7 connectivity through smart phones, the Internet, electronically enabled social networks, laptops, and emerging technologies have counter-intuitively increased human isolation while promising richer relationships. This unintended emergence of a new form of human isolation has further complicated human interactions and increased the stress in early 21st Century life. People have become more agitated, exhausted, impatient, and burnt out as they have succumbed to the addictive appeal of their electronic devices.

Clandestinely, the 21st Century offers the unsuspecting person a new type of addiction that reduces the quality-of-life by correspondingly dulling the intellectual sharpness of unsuspecting persons. Continuous and unrelenting connectivity has begun to reduce the range and depth of human intellectual life. Many people live with intellectual exhaustion without knowing that something is amiss. Moreover, society quickly accepts this new assault of intellectual fragmentation as the new norm of human excellence. The signs are everywhere. Look at your experience. Is everything O.K. with you?

In the workplace, technological events, like cyber terror, unexpectedly challenge executives and their managers. The landscape of social challenges is immense: Irresponsibility, conceptual confusion, terrorism, abortion, gay marriage, diversity, taxation, health care, government regulation, political corruption, and the growing challenge of economic well-being all impact management practice. These complexities, coupled with the pressures of business competition, seem to make the desire for a simpler life virtually impossible to achieve. Thankfully, life only seems this way. Many people have mastered the art of enjoying a simpler and more joyful life.

> **Simple Joy Principle One: The greater the complexity of human life, the greater the access to Simple Joy. — R. L. Newkirk**

Human beings can simplify the complexities of their relationships by adopting the values that make human life authentically human. Such higher values as simplicity, love, hope, truth, courage, beauty, and human growth contain the wondrous power to lead people in new directions whenever life becomes too complex to be comfortable. These values are the stuff of great dramas, and powerful stories have emerged through their telling. They are the foundation of our character as fully human persons.

Such values form one of the great paradoxes of human life. How can these values possibly be so potent and noble? We cannot easily define these values, measure them, or explain them. However, we know them, recognize them, are inspired by them, and seek to make them the core of our very intimate lives, even to the point of absolute self-sacrifice. "No greater love..." The most admired people live by these values. Everyone knows who these people are; even the small child is attracted to such people. These people are virtuous.

What are these values that they hold such power over us? We commit to them. We sacrifice for them. We dedicate and order our lives by them. We fight for them. Unquestionably, they inspire us to scale new heights. Where did they come from, these values that have changed the face of humanity? More importantly, how did these lofty values become such an integral part of our lives? Such higher values are implicitly accepted in a veil of ignorance, but are explicitly powerful enough to alter the course of our lives and the very rhythm of our hearts.

As finite creatures, we human beings forever remain unaware of the pull and tug of our values as they remain in the background of our lives, turning us this way and that. Without our conscious consent, our values influence and guide our very way of life. They simplify our lives as they lead us away from our most basic impulses for vanity, money, power, fame, popularity, intelligence, and success. They point the way to something more enduring.

From the background shadow of our existence, often beyond the grasp of our consciousness, constituting little part of our functional self-awareness, values exert a profound influence on the direction of our lives as their call for self-sacrifice carries us beyond the basic animal drive to seek deeper pleasures or basic survival. Intrinsic values, when we listen to them, release us from the existential basement of L1EH. Being a human being is really more than being a kangaroo or a Tyrannosaurus Rex. Higher values, when lived consistently, become the powerful forces of personal fulfillment.

The questions are haunting: Why live value-inspired lives? Why value a human life influenced by background forces that annihilate the natural drive to self-absorption? How is it that such intrinsic, and mysterious, difficult-to-measure forces are seen as the royal path to an inspired life? Such values are vital to us because they inspire new heights of human creativity. The values of simplicity, love, hope, truth, courage, beauty, and human growth guide us to greet each day in novel ways.

Through these values, we respond to the changing patterns of life by generating fresh advances in the art of living a genuinely human life. Through their hidden influence in forming our character, our higher values inspire us to lead a life of selfless devotion to higher principles which we may not even understand but, nevertheless, hold fast. Such values carry us well beyond the basic needs of our lives and free us of the imprisonment of L1EH to touch the higher realms of spirit that elicit spontaneous admiration for other people.

The silent promptings of our intrinsic values encourage us to pay a steeper price for the attainment of a fully human existence and the Simple Joy it generates. Responding to such promptings, we eventually discover the grand truths that matter most in life. Eventually these grand truths simplify our relationships by guiding our decisions.

Nevertheless, without completely understanding what these values are, their power over us, where they come from, or even whether they make sense, we become values-driven people who even pledge our lives to the cultivation of these mysterious forces that we steadfastly hold to be so sacred. This is not necessarily a good thing. The unexamined life is a life not worth living. I guess we ought to examine it.

A values-driven life is resilient. For example, when the higher values of their lives guide them, people in every walk-of-life see the way out of the unforeseen challenges that spring up all around them. This occurs through a spiritual prodding of these values which brings people to know more clearly right from wrong and up from down. Moreover, living such a values-inspired life enables people to meet the challenges emerging from the unexpected contingencies of life. Hence, they rekindle the meaning of their existence. This, in turn, enriches their relationships as they begin to see their way through the forest of complexity that haunts the modern world.

Guided by a more informed vision of the future, then, relationships enable people to more appropriately resolve important issues of the times. These workplace issues may include anything such as terrorism, government regulation, and economic well-being, as well as the pressures of business competition.

> **Academics may argue that the power of reason defines the human being, but it is our high values that make us fully human. — Raymond L. Newkirk**

Joyful Relationships at Work

The foregoing considerations naturally lead to an important question: What are joyful workplace relationships? They are Human Activity Systems that cherish reason, judgment and "Axiomatic Ethics". This is a term I created to highlight the changes in relationships that have occurred over the last decade. We are living during a time of simply wondrous history. The demise of Axiomatic Ethics has been one of the most significant challenges of 21st Century workplace relationships. It is also the stuff of many workplace relationships through which countless numbing meetings produce very little productive outcomes. Think about your own experience. I have met people who make a living by going to meetings to schedule other meetings.

Danger of Axiomatic Ethics

What is Axiomatic Ethics? Whatever it is, is it really in demise? If so, does it matter, really matter? Yes, it matters to relationships that produce great outcomes. A topic like the "Demise of Axiomatic Ethics" implies a workplace confrontation with virtue. This is a bit dangerous because the word "Virtue" cuts to the core of modernity and sparks suspicions of fanaticism. Think about the many issues that come to mind when you hear that management is going to do something about the problem of virtue in the workplace. Chilling, right?

Whose virtues matter at work? While some people may truly be more virtuous than others and the virtues of some people are vices to others. If management begins to advocate the acceptance and practice of a specific set of virtues, will anyone comply or take the request seriously? These are proper concerns. After all, business organizations are secular endeavors, not religious or philosophical institutions.

Obviously, the topic of virtue generates discomfort about what it means to be in a productive workplace relationship. Moreover, people already consider themselves to be experts on the form and substance of human nature. This includes the generation of human nature, its formation, development, maturation, life-cycle processes, evolutionary unfolding, transformation, hybridization, change, metamorphosis, life purpose, and growth. Probably experts have already written several thousand books and articles about workplace relationships. Obviously, early in the 21st Century almost everyone is a master of human nature. Ask them. Look at the world. No cause to worry.

Around the mid-1950s, following the "war to end all wars," people pretty much understood that certain things were not so good and other things were better. One of these things, of course, was a person's word. Your word and how you kept it was the measure of your character. A lie was always less desirable than the truth. Your handshake in a social transaction symbolized your character. That's it, period. Character mattered.

Ethics and morals mattered too. Most thinkers understood that ethics and morals separated us from the brute animals. The particularly human capacity to be moral persons rescued us from the threat of annihilation by members of our own species. Human beings were somehow different from the other creatures that shared this planet with us. At least, this is the theory.

As the years passed one after another, attitudes changed. Eventually people moved from handshakes to contracts, documents people often ignored. Discussions about values dominated Board Rooms while commitment to virtues became the concern of monastic communities. Eventually history moved into the 21st Century. This is all complicated stuff. It certainly complicates life at work for a great number of people who like to do things right.

The simple joy of relationships emerges from simple living. This means that relationships ought to encourage simplicity. This is great insight for building joyful relationships and to enjoy the fruits of Simple Joy. Voltaire, a really interesting European, reminded us that one has to laugh at life to get through it. He also had to flee France for the safety of another country because the pre-human beings in France who controlled everything there did not laugh much at life. Undeterred, Voltaire thought it was great to be criticized by certain people because it meant that he was not like them. Voltaire might not have lived a very simple life, but he was consistent in thought and action. For Voltaire, consistency was a virtue that emerged from self-care.

Voltaire understood that people are known more by their enemies than their friends. Voltaire must have laughed a lot in life, especially from the safety of other countries. He died back in France a big theatrical success. He threw his last play into the fire because the critics loved it. Voltaire was very sad that day.

Look at who liked his play. He ended up being liked by his critics and thought it was a bad thing. At least he was fortunate enough to have some critics; they helped him maintain his true direction in life. Fully human persons need some standards to illuminate the darkness. Critics provide those standards and add joy to relationships by keeping one humble. You see, joyful relationships wrap honesty and truthfulness in kindness.

> **A wise person loves his friends but values his critics more.**
> **— Raymond L. Newkirk**

Occasionally we will form relationships with people who prefer to get by without any kind of criticism. In fact, criticism of any kind is a formula for failure, they believe. Some organizations consider any form of criticism as discriminatory behavior. In these organizations, management views moral arguments as particularly aggressive and disruptive to the harmony of the environment.

The common management position today establishes a principle that I refer to as the Principle of Inverted Morality. It states that arguments guided by an appeal to morality are immoral. For them, a moral argument is de facto evidence of discrimination and, thus, immorality.

However, authentic "personhood", that is, a moral locus of rights, requires a person to render moral judgments in the conduct of human affairs. Moral judgements by definition are discriminatory judgments concerning moral acts and immoral acts. This concern for morality is a uniquely human capacity. It sets us free from the constraints of brute animal life.

The question arises, therefore: What is a joyful relationship? Can one ever be joyful in an amoral relationship? This is a trick question. What I am really asking you is this: Can you really be joyful living like a brute animal in opposition to your defining nature as a moral being? Sounds different when ask the question this way, right? However, it is fundamentally the same question.

Ideally, the answer is no because an amoral environment is one in which moral value does not exist. This is the natural state of brute animal life. Damn the torpedoes and full speed ahead. Up is down and hot is cold. Everything is relative. Actually, to be human means to be a moral being. One can never be truly joyful by ignoring the defining power that separates human beings from other living beings. Human beings, after all, are not cats, dogs, kangaroos or dinosaurs. Human beings are endowed with the deep capacity of moral behavior as a defining characteristic of their decision making.

Virtues in Moral Life

The question of morals naturally leads us into a discussion about the place and role of virtues in moral behavior. More importantly, the problem of virtues in human affairs is another one of those sticky subjects that cannot be long ignored without seriously eroding the "value" of human life itself. Naturally this is the case because virtues are both subjective and objective. Subjectively, everyone has their own values.

Many people who have their own values think that they should live by their values or not live at all. Objectively, there are values that everyone lives by; but people just take them for granted and live as if they do not matter when they actually do. In this way, some people can spend all of our time arguing with us over the subjective values that mostly do no matter to anyone but them.

Values are indeed argumentative because they are so vital to the substance of human fulfilment. We really need to get them right. Indeed, values are pivotal to human joy. There is no real joy without living a value governed life. The question, of course, is do I mean objective values or subjective values? In workplace relationships, it is important to get them right. Morals matter at work, so implicitly, values must matter also. For, the former follows from the latter. Probably almost everyone knows at least this much about values and morals. Morals are about the behaviors that follow from the values one holds dear.

Why does this matter? For one thing, we know that at work, unethical people, those who exercise immoral behavior, will run out the ethical people, those who exercise moral behavior. Crooks develop criminal organizations. Who really wants to be part of an immoral workplace relationship? Objectively, no one deliberately sets out to enter such a relationship. Subjectively, however, many people become involved in immoral workplace relationships because they become disconnected from their objective values and run free and loose with their subjective values as if nothing matters but them.

Moral people are quite different from immoral people in so many ways. If you think about it, you can see that the decisions people make reveal such differences very openly. Life is a journey of good decisions versus bad decisions. The Quality of Life rests in the balance between the two. Great people have a history of making good decisions while nefarious people have a history of making bad decisions. Think about it.

Fallacy of Strategic Relativism

Recently, strategic relativism has become the dominant "ism" of management thinking and practice. This has resulted in the "demise of axiomatic ethics" that normally informed the management thinking of ethically minded individuals. The banking crisis, housing crash, government irresponsibility, and business collapse bear witness to the loss of the ethical grounding that makes a free economic system function well.

For probably the first time in American business history, senior executives earned tremendous salaries and bonuses for getting it wrong. Not only did they get it wrong, they did what they did illegally. Nevertheless, the justice system, on instructions from the top, looked the other way when the depth of criminality became obvious to the investigators and regulators.

Strategic Relativism is a fallacy because it brings about its own destruction. Things simply quit working and markets die. Without being fully aware of the implications of their short-sightedness, many people have formed workplace relationships in which ethics have become less axiomatic and more relativistic. With this being the environment of the modern organization, we can wonder if the character of a relationship depends upon the character of the people who form it. One may well ask: What is the role of moral judgment in building character?

True, life has become more complicated for some people, but the past had its challenges too. Even in the 1960s, character was always on short supply. Unlike today, however, the axioms of ethical behavior were obvious to most people. Crimes led to punishment. Dishonesty led to censure. Handshakes counted as personal contracts.

People saw misbehavior as a process of bad decision-making that had to be rejected. They understood the implications of Mel Conway's Law: "The organization of an organization reflects the organization of the people at the top." I like to think that the character of an organization reflects the charter of the people at the top, in any organization.

The quality of human life rests in the balance between good and bad decisions. — Ray Newkirk

We will soon conclude this series by connecting the dots. We have discussed Moral Wisdom, Continuous Performance Management, Insider Threat Prevention Cyber Security, the Cardinal Virtues, the Newkirk Model, and the necessity of navigating the sociopaths at work. In the Continuous Performance Management organization, these topics fit together to deliver a unified model of team potency. Digital transformation radically modifies the design of enterprise architectures. Data, information, and knowledge are more accessible from nearly anywhere in the company. Programs such as Big Data and Data Analytics deliver a real-time view of business measurements through specially designed delivery platforms. The assumption, of course, is that the data, information, and knowledge are accurate enough to be useful in competitive decision making. Digital Transformation, Big Data, and Date Analytics is thought to deliver a united business operation.

Digital records enable managers to introduce new and more potent business models like CPM. However, Cyber Attacks such as those emanating from Insider Threats force organizations to modify these models by moving from open processes that integrate business operations to discrete platforms that unite Insider Threat Prevention Cyber Security strategies with the new enterprise models. Chapter Twenty summarizes the challenges of optimizing Insider Threat Prevention Cyber Security by navigating sociopaths at work using a virtues-based management approach.

2: Character

America misplaced a lot of character over the later years of the 20th Century as it became the center of global Capitalism. Generally, the under fifty generation is fundamentally unaware of how much national greatness has evaporated during their lifetimes. Indeed, even if you make the attempt to describe it to them and explain how character once mattered and why, many in this generation will not believe you or simply will react with cold indifference.

People in our great nation little understand that character is the cosmic portal to human freedom. Iconic people recognized for their greatness remind us that it takes character to live a life of freedom. We all have heard the countless stories about the value of personal character. A person 's word defined a person's honor. We are told that one's word and honor were the major currencies of a by-gone age. Indeed, the hand-shake signified life itself. People lived as if their honor was vital to their every aspiration. They worried about the "good name of the family" and keeping it intact.

The death of honor signified the very end of life itself. The brutality of life emphasized the necessity for character as the core determinant of an authentically human society. Civil society required civilized people. A man's word and honor made him civilized. It is unlikely that we will pass this way again. Now we have attorneys.

The message today is quite relativistic. Not only do handshakes matter less, but contracts are drawn up to be broken as evidenced by the hubris of professional athletes who demand new contracts before old contracts have expired or banks who change interest rates on existing balances because our "Congressional Representative" rigged the laws in their favor. It makes sense that this guy is running for President. Even the mafia treated people better this this in the 1950s. Today the legal system feeds off itself as the rights of civilized individuals evaporate in a cloud of green ink that had replaced honor as the mark of character.

> **A free person is a moral person: This proposition requires extraordinary insight to grasp. Without adequate reflection, it is difficult to accept. — Raymond L. Newkirk**

Freedom in Truth

Self-discipline makes human life potent. Even Freud acknowledged this much; although he used different language to explain it. The question arises, however, is what do I mean when I speak of moral character? It consists in the impulses and behaviors that make us really different than we would be without character. For example, when people lie, they are liars, at least in that instant. When they do not lie, they are not liars. Non-liars are really quite different from liars. An aspect of this difference is that they possess a familiarity with truth that the liars cannot claim.

The truthful individual possesses virtues that the liar has misplaced. Sure, everyone tells "white lies", and fib some. In fact, the art of telling a lie is the dominant defense mechanism of human beings. We all lie sometime. Occasionally, a lie can be a prudent act. When I speak of sociopaths at work, I am not referring to the prudent lies of kindness that saves the feelings of another person from hurt. I am speaking of the habitual lies of manipulation and annihilation that do real damage to colleagues, friends, and strangers. I am speaking about the lies of sociopaths, the habitual liars.

Nonreality of Habitual Liars

Have you ever observed that habitual liars forget about reality altogether? Indeed, liars even forget that they have become a "people of the lie". Habitual liars frequently believe their own lies so much so that truthfulness matters less every day. In time, habitual liars escape the bonds of reality and become incapable of perceiving the sad state of their existence. Indeed, they have relinquished the capacity to live a genuinely free life. Their lies now own them, really, not metaphorically.

These "people of the lie" have made themselves impotent beings who have swapped the shores of reality for the shackles of deception. Strangely, this can happen to anyone anywhere and anytime. We see it in virtually every walk of life. The price of human freedom is the attainment of moral character, but this requires effort. Many times, it is easier to lie and abandon moral character.

Newkirk's Principle of Human Freedom: Human freedom is directly proportional to moral character: The more character, the more freedom.

— Raymond L. Newkirk

Path to Freedom is Moral Courage

Character matters; and moral character matters even more. It is not by accident that habitual lying becomes the moral equivalent to self-annihilation. If you lie long enough and hard enough, with deliberate frequency, you become less than what you were before all the lies began in that pristine age when you walked in truth. Sadly, you may never return. Liars become desensitized to their own moral blindness and eventually see the love of truth as a weakness of character. Lies are expedient behaviors of the fearful.

Strength becomes weakness and weakness becomes strength, the upside-down world of the liar as liars refine their craft. Since the root of lying emerges from a dim and often unrecognized fear of personal loss, the liar renounces the freedom offered by moral courage and diminishes his or her potency to act with strength. Occasionally, through the lie a Pyric victory is won, but the inevitable battle for personal freedom is lost. Lies annihilate the human capacity to be free. Such is the case with every less than moral act. Humanity is weakened by a weakened humanity. Moral character constrains moral weakness, but such constraint is lost with people of the lie.

The philosopher Alisdair MacIntyre has argued that moral judgment is dissipating because we are losing the freedom to have coherent conversation about ethics. Additionally, we find that world opinions about ethical matters have become more diverse as the world rapidly shrinks. Moreover, the proliferation of the 24X7 media reduces the capacity of people to discern right from wrong. In some countries, we find that political correctness has replaced moral correctness. In universities and governmental organizations, we further find that moral arguments are now construed by some people as acts of aggression or micro-aggressions.

People make ethical objections (discrimination!) about the making of an ethical objection. This incoherent position raises significant danger in the workplace. If we have arrived at the point where we cannot discuss moral issues, violence becomes the only recourse we have in the adjudication of our disputes, either direct or indirect. The sociopaths of society have learned this lesson well. They are intelligent people who rarely exercise little moral judgment, a two base hit. If their immorality is an essential characteristic of their individuality, and they lack empathetic relatedness, they become the sociopaths we hear about in the news. We see this whenever someone frames a terrorist as the victim of self-radicalization.

Today, sociopaths and psychopaths are everywhere. We find them in criminal justice. We find them in schools. We find them in politics, where lying is the potent currency of sophistication. We find them in business. We find them in the military. We find them in religion. We find them in terrorism, where they can even kill themselves after brief episodes of self-radicalization. People have forgotten that the vitality of a moral life forms an essential aspect of living a fully human life. However, they can see very clearly how the lack of morality unravels the human person because the human personality has unraveled.

Have you ever noticed that the atmosphere feels a bit different around a sociopath? They are slick but scary, especially when you look them in the eye and know that they are planning their menu. The sound you hear around the sociopath is the vacuum created by the unnatural absence of morality. Deficits in character produce vacuums in the quality, direction, and development of life. The lack of morality impacts everything, especially how human beings exercise "the uniquely human capacity to reason rightly".

> **"Irrationality expands whenever morality is divorced from reason. It is irrational to deny the prominence of morality in forging a truly human life. In honor of Lady Truth, right reason emerges from Morality and refines both itself and morality throughout the cycle of life." — R. L. Newkirk**

A free person has no need of lies, manipulation, or coercion. A free person competes only with oneself. A free person is a moderate person who understands that the more you own, the more it owns you. A free person is a responsible person who understands that human beings are more important than ideas, and this is the most important idea of all. Thus, a free person is a moral person.

> **A free person is a moral person: This proposition requires extraordinary insight. Reflection clarifies its meaning. — Raymond L. Newkirk**

Watchword is WATCH

Granted the last paragraph sounds idealistic. Nevertheless, it has the ring of truth. Would it not be great if no one ever had to lie about anything? Of course that is never going to happen. A free person this and a free person that. How many people think about the Cardinal Virtues as the path to freedom? What does it mean to be a virtuous person at work, and everywhere else? What does this have to do with navigating sociopaths at work, Insider Threat Prevention Cyber Security, and Continuous Performance Management?

As we have seen, the Cardinal Virtues consist of Justice, Fidelity, Self-Care, meaning development of one's conscience, and Prudence. These are the fundamental virtues for building potent workplace relationships. They are seminal to the development of productive teams and successful Continuous Performance Management. The Cardinal

Virtues enable teams to become the WATCH – full contributors to the success of their organizations. They add substance to the human environment by:

- Guiding employees to watch what they say (W)
- Taking the appropriate actions (A)
- Governing their thoughts prudently (T)
- Making smart choices (C), and
- Mastering their hearts with empathy (H)

Obviously, people who practice the Cardinal Virtues have spent a lifetime becoming virtuous people. Other people, however, go through the motions and do the dance because they know how to manipulate their colleagues and teammates. Eventually, however, the duplicity evaporates and colleagues see that the emperor has no clothes. Virtuous people have the advantage of recognizing integrity when they see it. Sociopaths, however, see people as useful or useless, as marks or resisters. The Cardinal Virtues naturally separate the best among us from the worse among us. As you can see, though, this section raises a large number of questions about personal integrity. You can learn to answer them by mastering the Newkirk Model presented in this book.

As you begin to put everything together to build your map for navigating sociopaths at work, you will encounter a number of soft and hard-skills questions about the topics presented in this book. At such times, you can spend countless hours searching online for inappropriate responses or you can access the Deep Technology capabilities of Systems Management Institute's Applied Intuitive Solutions™ Platform.

3: CPM & ITP Framework

Thinking in Paradigms

While many people create new processes that improve entire industries, some people inspire new paradigms that change the world. Paradigm Changers differ from the process builders in several very significant ways. For one thing, the Paradigm Changers think differently. They search for the "First Principles" and "Ultimate Causes" of their objects of inquiry. Process improvers, however, seek out "Proximate Causes," the up close and ideas. They keep their feet on the ground and think more about the here and now.

The Paradigm Changers engage in extremely high-level abstract thinking. As highly intelligent people, Paradigm Changers understand the nature of thinking and have developed the habits of the will, the virtues, necessary to perfect it. Obviously skilled at making the abstract concrete, Paradigm Changers, displaying the Hallmark of Human Intelligence, enlighten others by bringing the lofty truths of the First Principles down to earth for the less lofty thinkers to understand them and be lifted up by them.

Paradigm Changers have cultivated the skills of reading and reflecting. They remember what they write and what others say about their writing. As deep thinkers, the Paradigm Changers study the different methods of thinking and observe the outcomes of each method. Moreover, the Paradigm Changers study the nature of perfection and apply what they learn about it to their lives. They work hard to practice what they preach as they employ simple exercise to teach others.

Adoptive Problem Solving

Have you ever heard the expression: "Nothing under the sun is new"? There is some truth to this bit of insight. People share the same problems and mistakes more often than you would ever imagine. People most commonly adopt the same, or very similar, solutions. If you take the time to look deeper, you will find that very few inventions, products, or insights offer anything radically new.

Out of a hundred proposals perhaps only two or three are genuinely innovative. It takes a lot of "something special" to launch a new paradigm. Uber is an example of a company that is changing the taxi business by offering a modified taxi business, not a new paradigm of people transportation.

A paradigm shift takes a lot of time. People might think that a new paradigm pops up overnight, but they would be wrong. Sometimes it just seems that way because it is so dramatic. Truth be told, a new paradigm takes at least a generation of innovative thinking to get things moving. When you look deeply enough, you discover that a paradigm shift requires a unique set of factors to come together in an unusually consistent manner. Along the way people adopt a systemic approach to expand the scope of understanding, enhance descriptive capability and problem solving.

The people who organize and validate the discoveries that pave the way to the emerging paradigms are most often clear thinkers who make connections among the conceptual innovations usually overlooked by most people. The paradigm emerges because the innovations that characterize the paradigm are:

- Universally applicable;
- Deliberate solutions to real challenges;
- Derived from inventive processes and principles, and
- Rooted in the deep technologies that impact entire societies.

Paradigms are powerful innovations that impact the course of human history in some profound way. The people behind the push for the new paradigm go through cycles of generalizing problems and their solutions and eliminating the contradictions they found in the challenges. Creative innovations often use scientific effects outside the field where they were developed.

Inventive Problem Solving with AIS™

The same general patterns of technical evolution emerge across industries and sciences as the same problems and solutions reoccur. Progress occurs as people redefine the nature of the problems they face. Rather than accept the situation merely as a problem to be solved, interesting things begin to happen when people begin to change how they see problems. For example, is a situation merely a problem to be solved, or is it an inherent or technical contradiction within the state of the situation that requires an innovative plan of action to leverage it for success? When we describe a problem as a "contradiction" we find that we can also predict creative solutions to that problem by following a number of powerful Principles that generate an "Inventive Problem Solving" approach.

This problem-solving approach enables people to identify the repeating patterns of problems and solutions while discovering the contradictions present in any situation. This deeper insight enables people to develop new ways or methods of using scientific effects and then applying the general Inventive Problem Solving (IPS) patterns to the specific situations that confront us. As we continually apply the IPS patterns, we eventually learn to generalize a version of the problem and its solution for future application.

Specifically, when using the AIS™ Inventive Problem-Solving approach, we begin by describing the challenge we face as an inherent or technical contradiction. Then, we re-state the challenge as a specific "How to" problem. From this specific problem description, we use the AIS™ Knowledge Base System to generate the solution that resolves the contradiction. We then apply the solution to our specific challenge as an action plan. The AIS™ Knowledge Base System is actually an intelligent repository of proprietary, evidence-based solutions compiled from global problem-solving practice.

Inherent and technical contradictions are at the root of an astounding percentage of problems. We can attain reliable solutions to many of these problems by eliminating the contradictions. Several decades ago, I referred to the inherent and technical contradictions as "quality versus anti-quality" tradeoffs. For example, a company may want an information system that is both user-friendly and extremely secure.

This created an inherent or physical contradiction back then because the only way you could design a user-friendly system would be by reducing its access security. One negated the other. Eventually, we solved this contradiction by redesigning the system's access architecture. We became very inventive. We learned how to separate the systems requirements according to the space constraints, time requirements, and the ability to scale.

AIS™ Framework for ITPCS

The AIS™ Framework assists ITPCS teams with eliminating the contradictions that reveal an organization's cyber challenges. Guided by the systems perspective, ITPCS teams apply Design Inquiry to build models of the Future System and the Knowledge Base System. They explore the system of ideas and problems to formulate the future system. During Inventive Problem Solving for ITPCS, we must examine the relevant aspects of the future CPM-ITPCS Unified System, its structure, environment, and processes. ITPCS teams can articulate the future environments of the unified system including its source, design and development, operations and management environments from the perspective of structure, behavior, and environment.

The Knowledge Base System (KBS) includes knowledge about the ITPCS system problems and ideas. This KBS obtains its knowledge from the environment of previous experience. ITPCS teams leverage the previous experience and current solutions from related environments to build new knowledge about the ideal end result and to find less expensive solutions using improved technical solutions. Throughout the Design Inquiry approach ITPCS teams continually searched for additional contradictions downstream thinking that solutions emerge from the elimination of contradictions. Following this path, teams look for the fixed patterns that predict the evolution of technology.

Integration of IPS & ITPCS

Many forces impact enterprise success. Along with the usual challenges, businesses today experience a strong shift in employee attitudes about work style and success. On one side of the management coin, employees prefer less management intervention and more self-direction. They want coaching and open environments with shared access to systems and information. They want an environment of trust. Leaders heard them loud and clear. They have responded to these expectations by delivering CPM, Continuous Performance Management.

On the other side of the coin, however, managers have experienced an even more severe challenge. The watch word here is "zero", meaning zero trust. The serious challenge of Insider Threat Prevention Cyber Security demands an environment in which everyone from the janitor to the CEO supports a rigorous program of Continuous Threat Management. Forget open access; forget pervasive trust; forget self-management, and forget an environment free from reviews. The Hallmarks of Continuous Performance Management and Continuous Threat Management seriously conflict.

It is obvious that organizations face both technical and inherent contradictions that require a range of potent solutions. Most likely these solutions will be expansive. Management may be forced to redesign the enterprise to protect its most valuable assets. Regardless of the approach contemplated, everyone will expect management to adopt the solutions that are most appropriate to each situation. In the following section, I elaborate a few Applied Intuitive Strategies to guide managers as they work diligently with their teams to secure the enterprise from Insider Threats and increase the effectiveness of their Continuous Performance Management operations wherever they can.

First, study the following strategies that assist with the adoption of the Applied Intuition Solutions. Next, using common sense apply the various suggestions in each strategy to the particular situation that you face. In several cases, the strategies appear to contradict one another. I caution that the situation only seems this way. They actually work in tandem to expand the range of possibilities of Insider Threat Prevention Cyber Security.

Employing Applied Intuitive Strategies

Strategy One, Segmentation or Decomposing to Micro-Level

Tight integration increases the threat level for a significant Insider Intrusion that impacts multiple systems, processes and information repositories. Over the last 35 years, systems and processes have become so tightly integrated, and coupled, that access to one that grants access to all. Unfortunately, tight integration often occurs in the Security Operations Center. Under the right situation, decomposing business processes or systems into non-integrated components can be a recommended ITPCS strategy whenever processes and systems remain easy to decompose and the state of decomposition increases the level of process independence.

As a rule, when these two conditions exist, management can decompose components wherever possible. Furthermore, management can restrict the size of software programs to improve testing saturation and software performance. Management may want to design information systems that employ applets. This kind of segmentation represents a sound ITPCS strategy wherever it can deliver a large number of ITPCS applications.

Today, Continuous Performance Management's inability to address the threat of Cyber Terror has made segmentation of the programs, data, systems, processes, and even business units an essential tool in the effort to protect the enterprise against malicious insider intrusions downstream. ITPCS increases the pressure on management to break large organizations into smaller business units or profit centers.

In a world threatened by Cyber Terror, smart management rethinks the enterprise model to ensure that a single employee cannot gain open access to corporate information assets. In today's business climate, a Cyber Security responsive enterprise becomes small, highly adaptable, but concurrently big enough to maintain productivity, sales, and economic growth. Insider Threat Prevention Cyber Security works best when an enterprise remains small while growing. Moreover, the proper use of proactive teams facilitates this enterprise segmentation design strategy by decomposing large jobs into smaller jobs.

Strategy One, Segmentation

Segmentation can become an approach to describe a system and identify a detailed set of problem statements. Here, teams can decompose a single problem statement into a collection of problem statements. Using this approach, organization can segment systems and applications to enhance the reliability of maintenance and facilitate Cyber Security. Segmentation becomes an approach that enables ITPCS teams to reduce a complex task into subtasks as large projects become smaller projects easier for individuals to monitor.

Strategy Two, Separation

Separate or decouple the nonessential and interfering components of a process or system from the essential components of the system or process. Define the criteria of separation such as frequency of use or critical nature. Focus Insider Threat Prevention Cyber Security on the essential components and processes.

This Principle reminds management to review the components of software and processes delivered by third parties and have them comply with ITPCS requirements to separate the nonessential from the essential and eliminate the conflicting specifications and requirements by pursuing the central purpose of the software. Eliminate all the unnecessary functionality.

Strategy Three, Ensure Local Quality

Redesign the internal structure of a process or system to increase variably. In a cyber terror world, not everything should be uniform. Design each part of an object or system to function in conditions most suitable for its operation. Design each component of a process or system to execute a different and useful function. Employ concepts of local quality to ensure that each segmented process or component reflects reasonable variability.

Local Quality is a broad Strategy that addresses concerns not only about business processes and systems but also about people. People are different and enjoy different work styles. This impacts Continuous Performance Management because may people do not respond well to team work. Some people are more effective working on their own. Since an enterprise employs people with deep technology specializations, the need for Local Quality applications becomes more pressing implementation concerns for ITP. Rethink hiring practices. Be careful of the lone wolf. CPM is not for everyone. Coaching may be insufficient for an ITP driven enterprise.

Ensuring that the local security of an environment is strong, change a system's structure and external environment from a uniform to a non-uniform design. Ensure that the system functions in the most suitable conditions. Ensure that each component of the system executes a different and required function. Use a separate system for each function.

Strategy Four, Symmetry Change

Change the design of the system or process from symmetrical to asymmetrical. If an object is asymmetrical, increase its level of asymmetry. Mass customization is a business strategy that corresponds to asymmetry, The business process, system, information file or even policies of an enterprise are specifically designed for each employee or customer and do not need to be the same as those provided to other customers. Design asymmetry into the environment.

Strategy Five, Merging

Merging often occurs as a co-strategy with segmentation. One enhances the other. Merge identical or similar objects whenever possible. Assemble identical or similar applications to execute parallel operations. Make operations contiguous or parallel. Combine them in time.

Management can secure the fragile and weak spots in ITPCS, such as open access to information systems, without increasing systems complexity by simply controlling access. Segmentation and merging are often more effective when implemented together. In this instance, management segments the organizations and then merges the parts of the organization. Using merging practices, small companies can grow while remaining small.

Strategy Six, Multi-Functionality or Universality

Using this strategy, companies increase the functionality of a process or system to simplify or eliminate other processes or systems. This enables managers to decrease the number of obsolete functions while retaining other useful functions. Management introduces universality to enhance the cross-functional skills of employees and to enhance the Local Quality strategy. Universality also decreases the number of people required to work on the system.

Strategy Seven, Nested Doll

Using this strategy enables designers to encapsulate one function inside another perhaps four to seven times. Designers and programmers commonly encapsulate file structures in other file structures.

Strategy Eight, Compensation

Occasionally, processes and systems become so complex that additional processes or systems are introduced merely to compensate for the complexity of the process or system. Designers use the Merge Strategy to enhance performance by simplifying the complexity of processes or systems and to better connect with the environment. Management may also use this strategy to simplify the CPM-ITP unified environment by introducing special purpose teams, engaging in process redesign, and otherwise flatting the enterprise to improve the Continuous Performance Management-Insider Threat Prevention Cyber Security collaboration.

Strategy Nine, Preliminary Counteraction

Organizations commonly implement processes and systems that deliver both harmful and useful effects simultaneously. Anticipating this, designers include Preliminary Countermeasures that minimize or eliminate these harmful effects. Moreover, designers create countermeasures that negate the undesirable stresses caused by the harmful effects in the mid and late stages of system's operations. Since organizations commonly resist change, including positive innovations, designers execute strategies that gain the involvement of affected teams and reduce the fear of the unknown.

Strategy Ten, Preliminary Action

Smart organizations are proactive. They develop solutions before people need them. Such organizations take Preliminary Action so that positive changes go into effect at the most convenient time without causing delays in schedules. Experienced teams have solutions ready to go even before people encounter the problems. Before customers ask, system design teams deliver solutions that deliver positive environmental impacts that satisfy ethical considerations of the Cardinal Virtues. In this way, they deliver a positive impact on the larger community.

Strategy Eleven, Beforehand Compensation

As organizations are never error free, some problems are more severe than others. This is a perennial problem for processes and systems of modern organizations. In the "AGE of ITPCS", experienced managers are well-prepared to respond to a number of serious threats. Their teams know where the problems are and they recognize which segment of a process or system is the least reliable. In response to this situation, these teams prepare emergency means beforehand to compensate for a system's low reliability. In response, management may post instructions to direct employees during emergency situations or they may implement a FAQ section on the company web site.

Strategy Twelve, Equipotentiality

Managers can employ this strategy to flatten the organization and reduce the political bad will associated with a hierarchical organization structure. Management may further employ this strategy to position team members at the same level to reduce the hierarchical behavior that may breed malicious insider behavior.

Strategy Thirteen, Inversion

Managers invert the action(s) typically used to solve problems in the Continuous Performance Management environment. Rather than bring in external consultants, go to them instead. Or, transition capable internal employees into a consulting role. Turn your organization upside down to get a handle on Insider Threat Prevention Cyber

Security. For employees who work at home, make the home office a part of the organization. Enable employees to generate their own solution plans using an Applied Intuitive Solutions Platform instead of waiting for consultants to find the answer for them at a heavy cost.

Strategy Fourteen, Curvature Dynamics

Increase the circulation of information to benefit team functions. Redesign workspace to increase the employee visibility. Increase visibility of restricted areas so that employee access can be completely guarded. Ensure that employee locations are monitored in rapid real time and that access is will-guarded by visible means.

Strategy Fifteen, Dynamic Components

Implement dynamic objects, processes, and systems that are designed to rapidly achieve optimal performance using self-regulation. Implement processes or systems that can attain optimum performance by responding to the changes in performance of the components of the processes or subsystems.

Decompose processes or systems into components capable of self-correction relative to each other. If a process or component is not adaptable, employ self-regulation processes to make it adaptive. Ensure that the processes or systems can change when the environment changes. Enable the organization to evolve into a flexible organization. Increase organization flexibility by adopting Segmentation strategies (strategy 1) and Flatter organization strategies (strategy 12). Also employ strategies to prepare changes before encountering a problem (strategies 9-11) and employ Discarding and Recovering strategies (strategy 34).

Strategy Sixteen, Partial or Excessive Actions

If 100 percent of an Insider Threat Prevention Cyber Security goal remains difficult to achieve after a first attempt using a specifically crafted solution, it follows that by using 'slightly more' or "slightly less" of the same solution, the organization may achieve a 100% Insider Threat Prevention Cyber Security solution.

Strategy Seventeen, Change in Dimensionality

Solve an ITPCS challenge related to a process or system by looking at the problem from multiple views. Malicious insiders may attack data stored in multi-dimensional arrays. The criminal may attack the data in one, two or three dimensions. Moreover, malicious insiders may attack whatever Intellectual Property is visible. On the upside, three-dimensional networks of business relationships respond to the needs of one member whose system is under attack more rapidly than one and two-dimensional relationships.

Strategy Eighteen, Access Governance

Engage in real-time access governance. Constrain the duration of access according to defined Access Rules controlling duration and number of accesses per person and number of persons per access.

Strategy Nineteen, Periodic Action

Instead of offering continuous access to sensitive files, employ periodic or variable access constraints per end-user. If an access is already periodic, change the timing sequence. According to nature of system, use pauses between instances of access to validate permissions during access for a single end-user.

Strategy Twenty, Continuity of Productivity

Execute workload continuously. Ensure that every component of process or system is consistently stable at maximum capacity. According to nature of system, redesign system to reduce or eliminate idle periods or intermittent operations. The rapid changes of digital technologies influence the application of Strategies Nineteen and Twenty. For example, the adoption of "Lean" and "Just-in-Time" operations favor the adoption of small, customized, production operations rather than large production operations of a common product.

Strategy Twenty-One, Deliberate Speed

Design processes that increase the speed of processing. Work smart, not slow. Conduct processes and transactions rapidly. Work fast to discover threats faster. Work fast to discover malicious insiders faster. Since speed is an asset in business success, work fast to discover threats fast. Since failures occur constantly, work fast to find failures quicker. Work fast to test more. Slow operations reduce the testing time of processes or systems that customers require. Enable project managers to deliver schedules that incorporate high-speed project delivery. Develop a pace based on the size of the job. If the work is big, break large projects into smaller projects to make high-speed manageable.

Strategy Twenty-Two, Fortunate Transformation

Turn threats into cyber intelligence. Use threat factors to strengthen Insider Threat Prevention Cyber Security processes. Transform potential harmful cyber effects within the systems environment into potent ITPCS solutions. Combine primary threat factors to reduce insider threats. Completely amplify severe threat factors to reduce the hidden dangers of the threats. Transform complaints and highly charged critiques into positive opportunities for Insider Threat Prevention Cyber Security expansion.

Use insider attacks on computer networks to generate information that improves ITP Cyber Security downstream. Use insider attack information to better protect systems and business processes from future attacks. Use the information gained from accidental insider attacks as a training library to prevent careless insider acts in the future. Use all information gained from insider attacks to develop strategies that protect systems and processes from future accidental attacks.

Strategy Twenty-Three, Feedback

Insider Threat Prevention Cyber Security is all about paranoia. It is about establishing responsive feedback and adjustment loops that have authority to act. ITPCS requires follow-through, cross-checking, reference checking to improve the ITPCS processes and specific ITPCS interventions. Management monitors the feedback and adjustment process to adjust the range and depth of its influence and ensure that the impact of the F&A process is appropriate to the challenge. Mature ITPCS processes employ virtual measurements to enhance on-line control. This will improve ITPCS by introducing the real-time metrics during the monitoring process. When properly designed and implemented, the use of real-time ITPCS metrics replaced post-facto inspections. ITPCS processes work best when management ensures that the F&A operations of ITPCS are continuously improved.

Strategy Twenty-Four, Temporary Solution

Use a temporary process or solution to prevent an insider attack until a permanent solution becomes available. If necessary, integrate or link the temporary solution with a previously existing solution to form an intermediary process. If possible, merge one solution temporarily with another until a permanent fix become available. Ensure that the temporary fix is easy to remove.

Strategy Twenty-Five, Self-Service ITP

Design an insider threat intervention process that manages itself in real-time, accumulates attack metrics, and executes actions that continually improve ITPCS. Use appropriate resources such as matter, energy, and information to enhance ITPCS. Store personal information about the criminal and the criminal's approach employed in the attack. Store the information in the ITPCS history system and include everything about the criminal from communities of interest and chat rooms to data exchanges. Track the frequency of insider attacks against the organization and use the decreasing success rate as the indicator of ITP quality. Realize that the more often an insider attack occurs, the lower your organizations rates in its ITPCS quality rating. These quality ratings represent information from human feedback and the systems self-assessment capabilities.

Strategy Twenty-Six, Copying

Instead of unavailable, complicated, expensive, or questionable ITPCS solutions, use simpler, inexpensive, solutions whenever possible. Replace an ITPCS system or process with an enhanced system or process and discontinue the earlier system or process. Continually update all ITPCS systems and processes. When developing new ITPCS interventions, run virtual simulations whenever possible including virtual simulations instead of actual team trials, video-conferencing instead of travel, and virtual reality to test new processes rather than in-house live tests that disrupt operations

Strategy Twenty-Seven, Cost Effectiveness

Reduce threat to primary system and entry to entire system, and replace an expensive, large system with multiple inexpensive systems without compromising Insider Threat Prevention CS.

Strategy Twenty-Eight, Human Monitoring

Replace human monitoring with sensor arrays. Use electromagnetic fields to interact with human actors. Use fields in conjunction with field-activated particles. Use infrared and wireless technologies to replace mechanical (wired) attachments. Employ new interaction technologies for real-time tracking and communications in sensitive areas. Transition monitoring processes to the micro-level for sensitive areas when appropriate.

Strategy Twenty-Nine, Environmental Fluidity

Design fluid work space to encourage the rapid generation of inventive ideas, Inventive Problem Solving, and accommodating alternative solutions to respond to fluid situations in Insider Threat Prevention Cyber Security. Implement flexible organization structure versus old fixed hierarchical structures to encourage openness in communications and human interaction. Design open spaces into the work areas to reduce conflict in high stress areas.

Strategy Thirty, Speed of Cyber Security

In cooperation with Strategy Ten, identify a process or system linked to the external environment that presents opportunities for attacks by malicious insiders. Improve the speed of ITPCS performance by appointing a person to shadow visitors who gain access to sensitive systems and information. Improve the speed of Cyber Security performance by assigning a single ITPCS specialist access to all the necessary data easily available so that inside actors gain access to only a single file of the organization's information assets, rather than every system file.

Strategy Thirty-One, Porosity

Continuously guard access to files. Secure the customer-facing layers of the company to safely filter the information flows both into and out of the organization. Secure these customer facing files against intrusion by malicious insiders using automated agents that shadow insiders who are granted continuous and temporary access.

Strategy Thirty-Two, File & Data Changes

Establish strict controls that prohibit visitors from changing files in any way. Establish strict controls that govern who, when, why, and how anyone can access and change files. Establish controls that constrain how anyone can change the data and information from the external environment. Change the transparency of a file or its external environment. Use this strategy in collaboration with Strategy Twenty-Five. Make activities of visitors transparent. Initiate standards of transparency when granting third party access to systems and files. Connections should be transparent for customers and employees. System should be impermeable for people who try to steal essential information.

Strategy Thirty-Three, Homogeneity

Have files that inter-act following the same security standards and procedures. People will more readily follow similar standards than standards that appear more challenging or less familiar.

Strategy Thirty-Four, Discarding & Recovering

Based on procedures, remove or delete obsolete files. Update out-of-date files and records during file maintenance operations. Conversely, restore useful file segments directly in operation as a component of production operations. Update the recovery processes according to schedule. Execute project completion procedures and discard expired files according to file maintenance standards. Ensure that security skills are transferable for future use. Eliminate security processes that are ineffective. Ensure that the organization updates and improves all Insider Threat Prevention Cyber Security work knowledge and skills directly on the job and during scheduled re-training.

Strategy Thirty-Five, Parameter Management

Insider Threat Prevention Cyber Security is all about change. Organizations change their systems daily. Insider Threat Prevention Cyber Security has to accommodate such changes in real-time. Change occurs in design of the systems environment and in the functionality and flexibility of software.

Change occurs in the relationships among systems and end-users. Technologies change, and standards change. In the ITPCS environment, business situations and policies change. Moreover, ITPCS must address the new flexibilities in employee relationships. Additionally, the adoption of mass customization systems also grants significant flexibility to insiders to plan new attack approaches that rapidly execute their criminal plans.

Strategy Thirty-Six, Phase Transitions

Phase transitions commonly occur among Insider Threat Prevention Cyber Security practices. Use phenomena occurring during phase transitions (e.g. volume changes, loss or absorption of heat, etc.). Many kinds of phase transitions exist. Ensure that ITP Cyber Security can secure the enterprise against the structural changes that occur such as mergers and acquisitions. Structural changes create a tremendous amount of confusion and require robust ITP Cyber Security practices to protect the organization during the common periods of disruption that are associated with structural change. Align the business processes and systems with new ITPCS strategies. Employ ITPCS practices to establish alliances with internal customers and employees. Discontinue all obsolete practices.

Strategy Thirty-Seven, ITPCS Expansion

Use expansion or contraction of Insider Threat Prevention Cyber Security to improve Cyber Security effectiveness. Use multiple ITP Cyber Security solutions with different requirements of organization coverage. Gain the buy-in of employees to expand ITP Cyber Security coverage and enhance the effectiveness of enterprise-wide ITP Cyber Security programs. Employ the CPM teams-based approach to increase ITPCS potency. Expand the internal marketing of ITP Cyber Security to increase employee awareness of the necessity for due diligence in protecting internal processes, systems, and operations against the intrusions of malicious insiders.

Strategy Thirty-Eight, Strong Intervention

Replace common practices with dramatic practices that prevent malicious insider attacks and uncover the malicious insiders that attempted to attack the systems environment. Update and replace the exposed system with highly secure software, standards, and security protocols.

Strategy Thirty-Nine, ITPCS Potency

Replace a normal Continuous Performance Management environment with one designed to leverage Insider Threat Prevention Cyber Security as a competitive force in the marketplace. Add Insider Threat Prevention Cyber Security components and Insider Threat Prevention Cyber Security functionality to every process and system. Implement an Insider Threat Prevention Cyber Security functionality that facilitates normal operations while securing processes and systems. Initiate Insider Threat Prevention Cyber Security operations that eliminate the negative and destructive actions of malicious and careless insiders. Initiate teams of examiners who can arbitrate the actions and intentions of careless employees who damage systems unintentionally.

Strategy Forty, CPM & ITP Multiplicity

Change from a single to a multiple Insider Threat Prevention Cyber Security approach to secure the Continuous Performance Management environment. Transform Continuous Performance Management and Insider Threat Prevention Cyber Security into a composite environment. Initiate a transformation program using multi-disciplinary project teams. Employ multi-media presentations to spread the word throughout the enterprise. Seek the commitment of involved teams. Build commitment for the composite architecture.

Define the values and virtues that will drive the Continuous Performance Management and Insider Threat Prevention Cyber Security Unification Program throughout the enterprise. Transform a loose Insider Threat Prevention Cyber Security environment into a tightly coupled organization. Where necessary ensure that composite processes and systems are maintained by business owners and Insider Threat Prevention Cyber Security experts.

Combining Continuous Performance Management systems with Insider Threat Prevention Cyber Security systems will improve both secure business operation and Insider Threat Prevention Cyber Security effectiveness. In Cyber Security, composite systems deliver effective performance to a wider audience. Applied Intuitive Solutions™ Problem Solving builds composite systems that perform better than single systems.

This concludes Chapter Three and our discussion about the forty strategies of Insider Threat Prevention Cyber Security. In Chapter Four, we take a deeper look at Applied Intuitive Solutions™ to learn how the AIS™ Platform offers such an attractive Return on Value. For ITPCS, we begin thinking about problem-solving situation using a five Phase approach. For initial convenience.

- Inception Phase
- Elaboration Phase
- Construction Phase
- Transition Phase
- Production Phase

The Initial Lifecycle of the Unified Process Organization along Content & Time

Phases must consider a wide range of activities and deliverables including the following:

- Core Process Workflows
- Business Modelling
- Requirements
- Analysis and Design
- Implementation
- Test
- Deployment
- Operations and SUpport
- Core Supporting Workflows
- Configuration Change Management
- Project Management
- Environment
- Infrastructure Management
- Iterations

Just remember, Insider Threat Prevention Cyber Security ain't for sissies.

4: Why AIS™ are Valuable

Putting Inventive Problem Solving on a Business Basis

Systems Management Institute spent nearly 50 years building its Applied Intuitive Solutions Knowledge Base. Through the evidence-based intelligence of our Applied Intuitive Solutions, the focus shifts to the generation of Problem-Based Solutions as a necessity for competitive success. Shifting from consulting and training to AIS, we place Problem-Based Solutions on a business basis. We ensure that problem solving, skills transformation and knowledge transfer endures. In the business environment, competitive relevance requires our Applied Intelligent Solutions to be business oriented, mission oriented, effectiveness oriented, efficiency oriented, reliability oriented, management oriented, productivity oriented, and improvement oriented.

Our Business Advantage

SMI offers Inventive Problem Solving that saves organizations millions of consulting and coaching dollars through the elimination of up-front sunk costs. For the enterprise, we are a quicker, simpler, more responsive, effective, efficient, and less expensive solution-oriented business partner. Our Internet Assistant Action Learning™ (IAAL™) process employs specially derived AIS™ and delivery technology. Through Inventive Problem Solving, we leverage the power of the Internet to provide attractive cost to profit ratios. Seeking the optimal ROI, Systems Management Institute has aggressively generated its global Knowledge Base of Applied Intuitive Solutions™ consisting of many thousands of solution plans. Empowered by state-of-the-art information technologies, we offer powerful Inventive Problem Solving as a foundation of our proprietary Internet Assistant Action Learning™ architecture.

We transform problem solving to empower people and enable strategies. — Raymond L. Newkirk

Competitive Uniqueness

Differing from the problem-solving methods that take months to execute, we deliver evidence-based solutions derived from the global experience of SMI. We offer the essential knowledge required to solve problems. We offer relevant evidence-based solutions derived from the demands of work and focused on the soft and hard-skills. Systems Management Institute delivers cost effective Inventive Problem Solving on a 24x7 basis. Our potent content populates a Knowledge Base System that spans 270+ problem areas.

"Successful Internet delivered intelligence immerses one in the Inventive Problem-Solving experience and provides opportunities to solve problems in a safe environment." — Ray Newkirk

SMI designs Inventive Problem-Solving Platforms. We believe that design is the missing link in Inventive Problem-Solving success. Leveraging our design experience, we employ design inquiry to explore the different solution generation environments and develop our many content domains. Through design inquiry, we evolved an eminently practical Inventive Problem-Solving architecture that delivers evidence-based solution plans in rapid real-time.

SMI and Social Cognition

We reflected on theories and discoveries in Social Cognition when designing our Internet Assistant Action Learning™ architecture. We studied Self-Discrepancy, Knowledge Accessibility, Agency Theory, Change of Standard Effect, Activity Engagement, Regulatory Models, Regulatory Focus, Regulatory Fit, and Regulatory Motivation.

SMI and Theory of Regulatory Fit

The Theory of Regulatory Fit is particularly important to the success of SMI's Inventive Problem-Solving methodology. Through this Theory, we recognized that a high level of regulatory fit with a client's regulatory orientation is important when building an AIS™ Knowledge Base System. For SMI, attention to regulatory fit delivers important benefits such as:

- Increasing one's strength of motivation;
- Inclining one toward distinct means for goal attainment;
- Encouraging one to evaluate decisions and goal pursuits more positively;
- Inclining one to imagine feeling better about a good choice and feeling worse about a bad choice, and
- Encouraging people to assign value to the object of a decision.

Our AIS™ is compatible with the variable goal pursuit means of Platform clients, from the eagerness means of promotion-focused concerns to the vigilance means of the prevention-focused means. Since value from fit positively impacts the quality of life, we add value by enabling clients to experience regulatory fit.

SMI and Problem of Motivation

Motivation perpetually challenges everyone, even the most motivated self-directed person. In on-line problem solving, motivation becomes an even more difficult challenge. As an Inventive Problem-Solving company, we understand the challenges we face motivating people to sign-up for and successfully apply our Applied Intuitive Solutions™ via our Internet Assistant Action Learning™ format. Guided by the theory of regulatory fit in Social Cognition, we designed our AIS™ Knowledge Base to reinforce the Member's decision-making process about Inventive Problem Solving through Systems Management Institute.

"When people use goal pursuit means that fit their regulatory orientation, they feel alert and energized. They feel good about what they have done. Regulatory fit adds value to a person's life."

— E. Troy Higgins

5: Inventive Problem Solving

Systems Management Institute maintains a Virtual Research Center (VRC) of technical, behavioral, contextual, hard, and soft-skills evidence-based solutions termed AIS™. Our Virtual Research Center consists of static and dynamic solutions guided by experience-derived knowledge cutting across a range of industries. Our VRC focuses on static and dynamic AIS™.

Static Applied Intuitive Solutions™

Static AIS™ consists of relatively unchanging and invariant solutions to challenges about individual, team, and organization performance such as found in the following questions:

- What should be the goals of individuals and teams in my organization beyond any particular function or project?
- How does a manager face the certainty of failure and the uncertainty and insecurity of individual or team commitment?
- What is the use of struggling and competing if change is the inevitable end?
- What ethical principles should form the basis of comparison for all value judgments regarding performance of staff and professional relationships?

Answers to such soft management questions take the form of value statements and prescriptions for management behavior. Managers cannot arrive at empirical solutions to these questions like those available in the hard sciences. These categories of questions are better understood as value questions. As such they are the most important kinds of questions that managers can ask. If taken for what they are, value questions, they become meaningful and resolvable.

Authentic management success, for the duration of a career, emerges from the answers given to such "soft" questions. Failure to ask questions like these often has a paralyzing effect on the deeper development of the manager's intellectual and emotional life, and constrains the performance of the manager's team. Although not derived from verifiable knowledge, practical answers to these soft questions are based on the best verifiable generalizations or qualitative answers experience has so far produced. The data from which the ethical generalizations emerge must be explicit. Static solutions are, by definition, applicable by every manager and need not be devised by each person using them.

Dynamic Applied Intuitive Solutions™

At the dynamic level of practical actions, people do not seek answers that apply in general, as with the static or qualitative solutions above, but seek methods for getting solutions to very specific problems such as found in the following questions:

- How can I get my manager to increase his confidence in me?
- Who should I support on my team to jump start by project?
- Shall I purchase a new computer system or hire new people?
- How can I keep from blowing up when my team mate lets me down?
- How should I tell my employee that I am unhappy about his or her performance?
- When should I tell my employee that I am unhappy about his or her performance?

For these kinds of questions, our AIS™ offer evidence-based content derived from successful problem-solving experience around the world. Today, our AIS™ offer a Deep Technology that enables Inventive Problem Solving to rapidly deliver enduring solutions in diverse cultures. This is the quantitative dimension of our AIS™ Research Center. All value judgments at this level should, of course, remain consistent with and derivable from the more general ethical standards presented in the Static AIS™.

Unlike Static AIS™, you can apply Dynamic AIS™ to each situation. However, only people involved in the current problem situation are best prepared to apply Dynamic AIS™. Systems Management Institute has made every effort to generate AIS™ that resolve challenges involving feelings, thoughts, and actions. In this respect, our AIS™ become "patterns of proper evaluation and response." Success depends on competencies: Technical, Behavioral, Contextual, Hard and Soft. Our AIS™ addresses each one. What We Do: Systems Management Institute Delivers AIS™ that:

In Performance, we employ AIS™ to assist in improving:

- Business process performance
- Business process management performance, and
- Organization performance.

In Maturity, we employ AIS™ to assist in achieving:

- Business process maturity,
- Business process management maturity, and
- Organization maturity.

How We Do It: We Deliver AIS™:

- Enabling performance improvement and compliance
- Improving key metrics such as cycle-time, resource management, wait time
- Identifying and managing the constraints such as the bottleneck activity or resource management
- Exploiting the constraints such as leveraging behaviour, performance bottlenecks, or impedance
- Improving upstream performance
- Elevating constraints by leveraging business investment in the early, mid, and late stages of ITP projects
- Reducing constraint inertia by removing complex challenges

that endure

What We Deliver: We deliver AIS™ that:

- Builds ITP value
- Improves processes
- Builds ITP and organization maturity
- Links people with technology
- Builds the Human, Information, and Organization
- Capital to inform People and Technology
- Value generates cash flow
- Processes enable value
- ITP coordinates Processes
- ITP shapes and is shaped by organization maturity
- Maturity is determined by people and technology.
- Human Capital, Information Capital, and Organization
- Capital Inform People and Technology.

Systems Management Institute delivers AIS™ guided by the principles that:

- Value generates cash flow
- Processes enable value
- CPM coordinates Processes
- ITP shapes and is shaped by organization maturity
- Maturity is determined by people and technology.
- Human Capital, Information Capital, and Organization Capital Inform People and Technology.
- Success depends on CPM-ITP competencies: Technical, Behavioral, Contextual, Hard, and Soft.

•

Systems Management Institute enhances CPM-ITP Maturity by providing the Inventive Problem Solving that assist organizations with:

Balancing ITP with CPM business strategies

Managing the link between CPM-ITP maturity by addressing:

- Strategic Alignment
- Governance
- Method
- Information Technology
- People
- Culture

In Strategic Alignment, we deliver AIS™ that facilitate:

- Process Implementation Planning,
- Strategy and Process Capability Linkage,
- Process Architecture,
- Process Outputs Measurement,
- Process Customers and Stakeholders.

In Governance, we deliver AIS™ that address:

- Process Roles and Responsibilities,
- Decision Making Processes,
- Process Metrics and Performance Linkage,
- Process Management Standards,
- Process Management Controls

Management Systems consist of:

- Planning and Control Systems,
- Management Information Systems

-

In Method, we deliver AIS™ that address Process:

- Design and Modelling,
- Implementation and Execution,
- Control and Measurement,
- Improvement and Innovation,
- Project and Program Management

In Information Technology, we deliver AIS™ that address:

- Process Design and Modelling,
- Process Implementation and Execution,
- Process Control and Measurement,
- Process improvement and Innovation,
- Process Project and Program Management

In People, we deliver AIS™ that address:

- Process Skills and Expertise,
- Process Education and Learning,
- Process Collaboration and Communication,
- Process Knowledge, and
- Process Management Leadership

In Culture, we deliver:

- Process Values and Beliefs,
- Process Attitudes and Behaviors,
- Responsiveness to Process Change,
- Leadership Attention to Process, and
- Process Social Networks.

Enterprise ITP consists of:

- ITP for Management Systems
- ITP for Operational Systems
- ITP for Business Processes

Operational Systems consist of:

- Operational Information Systems
- Goods and Services
- Money

In Inventive Problem Solving, we deliver AIS™ Functional Solutions for:

- Strategy and Governance
- Contracting & Purchasing
- Receiving, Warehousing & Shipping
- Invoicing, Auditing & Accounts Payable
- Marketing & Sales
- Accounting, Billing & Accounts Receivable
- Support Processes for Human Resources
- Information Technology & Quality Assurance & Control
- Security, Safety

Business Activities lead to process groupings which lead to:

- Core processes,
- Business process flows,
- Operational process flows,
- Details process flows.

Systems Management Institute

- Defines the goal of our AIS™: Inventive Problem Solving, Skills Building, Performance Improvement or Compliance?

- Defines the key metrics: Cycle Time, Wait Time, Resource Utilization
- Identifies the constraints: Bottleneck Activity or Resource
- Exploits the constraints: Improve Behavior Creating Performance Bottleneck or Impedance
- Subordinates to the constraints: Improves Upstream Throughput
- Elevates the constraint: Invests to Improve
- Avoids inertia: Start the Process Again

Conclusion

By Now you should know how to navigate sociopaths at work. This book introduced a few of the experience, observations, and insights I have gained through the course of my career, a career that spans nearly six decades. I have seen a lot; I have learned a lot, and I have accomplished a lot. As we all know, it is hard to be human. Life is paved with heavy disappointments and great successes. In the midst of these ups and downs are, of course, human beings.

It is hard to be human, definitely. We need one another, but we should not be needy of one another. Reflect on the Cardinal Virtue of Self-Care. It is important to develop one's conscience. In a very substantial way, it is the other person that gives meaning to our lives. Think about it. No one is an island. We do things with people, for people, through people, because of people, in spite of people, and even to people. We share a people-centric existence. Even monks share this with us.

This work has delivered a model of human behavior based on what I term Existential Hunger. Here I describe how we develop from basic self-concern to a state of spiritual awareness of ourselves and other people. We have seen that we grow from and move to deeper experiences that should enrich our lives. We have also seen that some people become fixated and develop different attitudes about the place of other people in their lives and the role they serve. These people are fixated. They experience conflicts of growth. The world for them is all about Ego and getting what they want. For them, self-esteem is rarely authentic and empathy is a weakness that can be faked for strategic gain. These often become the sociopathic people we need to navigate at work.

This work links the need to navigate the sociopaths at work with Insider Threat Prevention Cyber Security because Continuous Performance Management, a widely adopted, organization model adopted throughout the world, advocates an environment of openness and trust. Without linking CPM with ITP more directly, sociopaths at work can become very creative and learn to leverage the organization in completely novel ways. We have described the Hallmarks of CPM and ITP and defined strategies for linking them appropriately. We have also learned that sociopaths can become quite successful when the goals of an organization and the goals of the person align, depending on the drive of the sociopath.

The key to navigating sociopaths at work is to decide whether you can work with them on a reasonable basis. While some are highly functional people who have achieved notable success, many more are disruptive to the lives of the people around them. This work presents two questions you should ask yourself:

- Are they the kind of people you should form relationships with at work?
- Are you the kind of person people should form relationship with at work?

This work provides useful insights into the challenges facing employees in the modern digitally transformed organization. With every organization facing the continuous threat of Cyber Terror, Directors, executives, managers, and employees have to become smarter, more aware of their surroundings, and sensitive to the attitudes and behaviors of team mates. This demands deeper insights into managing organization models such as CPM and technical architectures such as ITP and deep wisdom about navigating sociopaths at work.

SMI means something special by "Virtual Problem-Solving". We mean a Mobile Platform of relevant, practical, and specialized Applied Intuitive Solutions™ delivered through a Rapid Solutions Mobile Platform™. The RSMP™ has the following characteristics:

- Delivers solutions that support core workplace competency;
- Requires adequate validation through previous practice;
- Requires an architecture that integrates life experience with self-reflection, assuming intellectual and personal maturity, and
- Demands committed effort upon the industry, initiative, and desire of the client to resolve a challenge rapidly." — Raymond L. Newkirk

"Intellectual Capital is our most important asset. It is our new economic environment." — Raymond L. Newkirk

6: Rapid Problem Solving for a Busy World

As a multi-functional, and content heavy, evidence-based person, I have written blogs, led Forums, delivered Podcasts, authored books, developed the AIS™ problems-solving environment, and so many other things too boring to mention. What I have learned throughout all of this is how difficult life can become for some people who just "don't get it". So many things happen in life and sometimes very quickly.

When I was a younger person, many years ago, I had a manager who constantly told me, "He who hesitates is lost. Speed is the goal of everything." Since he was not a track star, I often wondered why he was always in such a hurry. He had no time to think about what had to be done. "Just do it, he would say. Who cares about the method? Method is madness!" Ouch! Imagine that. What a philosophy for living life. Don't look up and down the street before crossing, it slows you down. What a Life Philosophy. Simply amazing. There has to be boundaries to such management wisdom. And there are. Let's think about the Paradox of Problem-Solving. Do you know what this is?

The Paradox of Problem Solving

We want carefully designed solutions that solve specific problems rapidly, no doubt. Unfortunately, we cannot always get what we want. Some problems in Astrophysics have not been solved even after 50 years of working on them. When one considers the nature, age, and size of the Cosmos, this does not surprise anyone. Does it? Even today, a number of Astrophysicists are rewriting their ideas about the nature of the Cosmos because of the emergence of several great telescopes, the James Webb Telescope and the Vera C. Rubin Observatory which features the world's largest digital camera designed to deliver extremely detailed, high-resolution views of the Cosmos. This Observatory has already begun to reshape our understanding of the size and depth of the Cosmos. You see, progress can take time because it requires solutions from many disciplines that eventually come together to offer new insights to the nature of powerful problems. "And, so it goes." This is the world we live in. Some solutions demand a lot of work and plenty of time to eventually emerge. Hurrying up is not a problem-solving strategy. What is a strategy, however, is learning to design a solution strategy that can eliminate and/or combine several steps into one potent step. This is what I have done for many decades now.

Applied Intuitive Solutions™

The Applied Intuitive Solution™ is the result. Here, I learned how to reduce the problem-solving process from six or eight steps to one or two and obtain the correct result every time. No kidding! It can be done. Interesting, right? So, over a number of decades, I actually learned what that manager meant. If we expand and deepen our problem-solving thinking about problem-solving, we can speed things up nicely. Imagine going from six or eight problem-solving steps down to one of two!

I feel better already. Everything depends on using the right Theory. Theories make a difference. That's the ticket laddie. Thanks Scottie. So, this is the Theory. But we are not quite there yet. A little bit more needs to be clarified to make a genius of my manager from long ago. We have to think about how we arrive at and explain our "truths" and ideas, and visions, and insight, and so on.

Let Me Explain Myself Here

Have you ever had someone ask you to clarify yourself after saying something that you thought was very profound and clear? Not only did you have to tell someone something about something that confused him or her, now he or she had the nerve to tell you to explain what the heck it is that you just now said. "Of all the nerve!!" Give in an inch and they will take a mile.

The problem here, of course, is that explanations are often confusing and go way beyond what you originally thought was "enough said". So, what do you do? I guess the answer here depends on two things. In the first place, do these people deserve an explanation of something that was so obvious to you when you shared it with them. Secondly, are you Wise enough, experienced enough, grown up enough, knowledgeable enough, and most of all kind enough, to deliver a proper "Explanation" that will resolve their outstanding issues and clarify their confusion? Hold on here. I still have another question about this situation, which I do not envy: What exactly is a proper Explanation?" Will you please explain it to me?

The Chain of Meaning - Are We Lost Yet?

Some people had a problem. They asked me to assist them with it. After thinking about it for a bit, I decided to respond positively to their request. Then, I employed a specific Theory to form some relevant information that would resolve their situation, so I thought. Following this, they then asked me to clarify this explanation by explaining further. This naturally led to a discussion and some arguments about the meaning of my explanation about the previous explanation and whether any of this has anything to do with their situation that they desperately want to escape.

To help them out, I explained to them that explanations should be rigorous because they emerge from a range and depth of Theories that clarify the essence of explanations for everything imaginable, even their situation. Now, this made them feel better. They understood quite clearly now that I was also lost and needed help so they suggested that I work with them to find someone who could use the most appropriate Theory for explaining and solving their situation. So, when I told them that I am well versed in the Philosophy of *Science* and am the person who knows probably all of the Theories of Explanation and that the problem here was that they have yet to tell me their problem so no Theory of Explanation could help them, yet.

They were so impressed with this information that they told me that they would have never bothered me with their problem if they had known that I was so qualified in the Philosophy of Science and thus Theories of Explanation. So, they asked me if I could recommend someone who could help them as a consultant? They would be willing to pay for that person's assistance. Now they tell me. If I had only known that they were willing to pay for the assistance, I would have certainly been able to assist them.

All joking aside, can you see what I am getting at here? Problem-Solving is an adventure that has an intriguing history. Obviously, some people are better at it than others. Also, there are many approaches to problem solving for those who care enough to use a rigorously defined approach. There are probably as many approaches to problem-solving as there are people on Planet Earth, right Houston? Just because this may be true, it does not mean that this is a good thing.

There are only a few approaches to problem-solving that make logical sense. Doubtlessly, the illogical approaches to problem-solving are the most common. Although the need to solve problems is universal, as a tribute to human nature, the skill of solving problems is not nearly as universal. At the center of it all, is the need for explanation. It is at the center of all progress. Can someone explain to me why explanation is at the core of knowing as knowing is at the core of being for human beings?

The Value of Explanation is Exponential

How many times in your life have you asked someone to explain something to you? I bet more than one hundred. How well did the explanations serve you? Joseph Pitt (1988) tells us that:

"explanations are supposed to tell us how things work and knowing how things work gives us the power to manipulate our environment to achieve our own ends, and (2) science is supposed to be our best means of generating explanations which satisfy the criterion of providing the means to accomplish our goals." This is indeed very interesting. For Pitt, and many others, explanation is superior to knowledge. Lacking explanation, progress falters. So now we have moved from the search for explanation to the drive to attain and apply the best explanation. We have moved from knowledge to justification, and from this to explanation and then on to the Best Explanation.

Wow! Can you see how complex my obvious **"Chain of Meaning"** has become in the search for knowledge, wisdom, and correctness? Explanation is superior to knowledge although we use explanation to clarify the knowledge that proceeds it. This is the stuff that matters to us. I guess there is some wisdom in this, but someone needs to explain it better. However, if I tell you that explanation is superior to knowledge, am I not sharing some knowledge with you about the relationship between explanation and knowledge to make the claim that explanation is superior to knowledge? How does one explain this? I guess that this must be self-evident where no explanation is necessary.

Did I just make a self-evident statement? Or does someone need to explain it to me? If this is how Science operates, imagine what this can do for politicians. Simply amazing. Do you understand what I am saying or do I need to explain it? If I do not need to explain it, it must be self-evident. If it is self-evident, then other things must likewise be self-evident. Therefore, since I do not require explanation here, it is now obvious that the right kind of knowledge simplifies the cognitive demands of life.

Obviously, the test of any knowledge that we may possess is the explanations we form about this knowledge; but isn't explanation knowledge? Without these explanations, the knowledge of it alone is meaningless to us because it is our explanation of it that reveals whether or not we understand it correctly. After all, our explanation could be in error. Fo example, if I tell you that your fancy automobile can run on water rather than gasoline, I either know what I am talking about or I do not. My explanations can be in error. So, Houston we have a problem! Do you trust me enough to load up the tank with good old H^2O? No, I did not think so. You are an intelligent person. Can you explain your decision? Thanks. I now know what you were thinking all of that time. Explanation matter.

The Cosmos of Explanation

The challenge to explain all knowledge is an "Unending Journey". After all, we always have something to learn about something. Obviously, knowledge is everywhere people exist. Perhaps some animals share their species knowledge with one another. Some animals appear intelligent in some ways about some things. For human beings, explanation is center stage in the challenge of learning. With this being the case, we do ourselves a service by learning everything we can about the process and substance of explanation. What kind of knowledge is it that cannot be explained by anyone at any time? It must be like that stuff produced by a bull.

We know a lot of stuff about a lot of stuff. Is it knowledge simply because we know it? People use a lot of words for knowledge. Knowledge can be an understanding of something, especially a science, a fact of experience, a method, process or technique. It can be reflective experience, awareness of some facts or experiences, personal information and understanding, fact gained through reasoning and cognition, having information, that which is known, collections of targeted information, life principles of humanity, body of truth. As I stated, we know a lot of stuff about a lot of stuff. But, can we explain what we know? Can we explain the stuff we know so that being knowledgeable enhances our ability to form explanations. It is fair to say that we LL live in a Cosmos of Explanations.

Master of Your Fate

This relationship between knowledge and explanation clears the way for understanding the formative. conceptual organization of explanation and its connection to knowledge. Perhaps, explanation accesses knowledge to deliver an understanding which is the foundation of wisdom. Thus, we can see that explanation transforms knowledge to deliver understanding. So now we know what processes we employ to increase our intelligence, skills, and capabilities. Now we are at the place in this wisdom mystery to examine explanation more deeply to better understand how we can leverage explanation to become wiser people.

Uncovering Explanation

We the people examine the process of Explanation from several focused perspectives which, in time, have become the significant Theories of Explanation. Although there are a bunch of theories about Explanation because humanity is still creative, only a few have become the most commonly advocated and studied. They are a continuously evolutionary body of thought. As a Philosopher of Science, I have been studying the Problem of Explanation for a number of decades. It never gets boring. It grows and then shrinks and then grows again and then shrinks again like a living being. So, the ancient question endures: What makes an explanation satisfactory? In the Philosophy of Science, our deeper understanding of the Problem of Explanation crosses many boundaries. You only need to read the next few pages to get a better idea of how broad this topic can become depending on a person's interest and point-of-view. I will present a short review on the next few pages to give you some idea of how complex a seemingly simple idea can become with some conceptual fuel. Knowledge and explanation go together like cake and ice cream. You just cannot eat it. But, learning it would be helpful as you weave your way through the many jungles of knowledge.

Explanatory Unification

Where do we go for answers? Philip Kitcher (1981) suggested a way out of the existential mess as he points out that we have many questions about explanation. I must say that as a Philosopher of Science, I also recommend that we can go to science for answers. In this case, we can engage in conceptual reduction by reducing unfamiliar phenomena to familiar phenomena. Here, we can be less subjective. Some people refer to this as Explanatory Unification or finding the familiar within the unfamiliar. The goal here is to move away from move away from the intuitive or subjective category of understanding to adopt a more objective category of insight possible through a more systematic process of unification.

In this way, we move from a subjective process to a more objective process. Thus, in this way we strive to understand the common underlying structures and also processes that satisfy targeted or specific and testable fundamental principles of explanation. Some people commonly refer to this more scientific approach to explanation as Explanatory Unification. Theories of Explanatory Unification reason that a proper explanation binds disparate phenomena together within a single framework as we reduce the independent facts that require explanation. Unification Theories commonly see explanation as central to unifying disparate phenomena.

Theoretical Explanation

In the world of Theory, we have Hempel's Deductive-Nomological Model of Probabilistic Explanation. This Model employs scientific laws to inform deductive reasoning.

Explanatory Pragmatism

If Unification falls short, some people prefer a kind of pragmatism as their approach to explanation. For them, this means that explanations are not propositions, arguments, possibilities or even potentialities. In this view, an explanation is indeed an answer (Bas van Fraassen, 1980).

Scientific Understanding of Explanation

An early and influential model by Carl Hempel posits that a scientific explanation involves a sound deductive argument where the phenomenon to be explained (the explanandum) logically follows from true premises (the explanans), at least one of which is a law of nature. Got it? Sonds scientific to me since it affirms "a law of nature". While there is some agreement about the best model for scientific explanation, debate continues about that question whether explanation is distinct from scientific description. Such debate also questions the nature of the fundamental purpose of explanation within scientific investigation.

Illocutionary Explanation

In this perspective, explanation is seen as an "accomplishment" term (Zeno Vendler). When is it not? Explaining is an Illocutionary Act (Austin, J. L., 1962). While an accomplishment term refers to an act far different from an Illocutionary Act which refers to an act of explaining or even commanding or directing someone about something. Explaining may require span of effort that exceeds the span of achievement. One is present tense the other past tense. One is completed the other is ongoing.

Logical Explanation

The Logic of Explanation emerged from Empirical approach to scientific investigation. This is where the facts derived from hard evidence is everything. "Just the facts, mam, just the facts." Here we are seeking a logical explanation to some empirical situation. We are interested in explaining the what and why of things in a measurable way. It is only logical Spoke that we want to explain the following:

- What happened?
- Why did that happen?
- How many times did that happen?
- What made it happen?
- What made it stop happening?
- Here we need to clarify, clarify, and clarify what we can exhibit.
- In short, we want to know what happened, why did it happen, what did it impact, and how much did it impact it and for how long and what made it stop?

Non-Causal Explanations:

Non-Causal explanations, represented by mathematical and/or structural explanations, challenges the singularly causal explanations.

Statistical Explanation

If I decided to present a detailed explanation about Statistical Explanation, I would require about 60 to 70 pages to adequately introduce the topic. It is not so much that the topic is so complicated, it is that there is so much knowledge to discuss and information to share with the reader. This category of explanation is about events, classes, probabilities, properties, subclasses, members, specification, entities, qualification, provisions, arguments, and so forth. It is indeed a statistical explanation.

Causal Explanation

Wesley Salmon's causal models, which focus on the causal processes and physical connections between events. Causal Theories, including Salmon's, require that Causal Explanations must absolutely involve actual causal processes or connections between events. These Theories cannot rely solely on logical form or statistical relevance. We understand that causal Explanations often focus on identifying the underlying mechanisms. The science argument about cause and effect being what it is certainly addresses the influential role of causation in explaining the "what is it" of knowledge.

So, let me ask you, do you accept that every scientific explanation absolutely must be causal? If you say yes, not everyone would agree. If you say no, not everyone would agree. However, it is a fact that a few theories still strongly reason that we do best when we identify causes to explain phenomena even though we are aware of the many unobservable components that exist and contribute to the development of explanations. Simply think about physics and its reality of atoms, genes, gravity, and other components of reality. Perhaps this is why some people become pragmatic and favor theories of common language and therefore turn their attention to the communicative and cognitive dimensions for explaining knowledge. focus on the communicative and cognitive dimensions of explaining knowledge. People are different and so are their explanations for knowledge.

Pragmatic and Cognitive Theories

These Theories of Explanation move from the focus on Logical Structures of explanations to their communicative and/or cognitive functions. While the more common language theories emphasize explanation in building understanding between individuals, the more intellectual Cognitive Science approaches to explanation view such explanation as fundamentally a cognitive activity that produces fully mental models.

Predictive Explanation

Hempel liked reality as it was experienced. Going beyond experience made little sense to him. In this, he was not sympathetic to the ideas of Duhem. Hempel was all about gaining predictive control over one' future experiences. Scientific Theory only had value whenever it could be shown to have the capacity to deliver predictable future experiences. Hempel reasoned that two types of explanation make sense, the 'deductive-nomological' (DN) and 'inductive-statistical' (IS). They have the same structure. However, while the DN explanations deliver universal generalizations, the IS explanations deliver statistical generalizations. It is worth noting that not everyone went along with this. As to be expected, Hempel enjoyed his share of criticism. For some people, his ideas lack relevance.

Legalistic Explanation

Legalistic Explanations are attention grabbing statements that follow strict rules and standards for expressing the defining characteristics of a Legalistic Explanation. They imply the rules that guide the formation of such explanations. The rules are identified as strict, excessive, and literal. Unfortunately, they are not a walk in the park. They can be pure drudgery. Such explanations are formed through strict, extremely excessive, and unusually literal "adherence" to a governing set of guiding rules which confuse nearly everyone. Even me. I have studied English, Latin, Spanish, Russian, Arabic, Italian, French, Greek, Tagalog, and probably one or two I have forgotten. Oh, now I remember one more! I also studied "Technoease." That was really a brain buster. Often, Technoease just did not compute with me. Apparently, it lacks transformative meanings. WOW! Imagine that! Does that compute?

For the record, Legalistic explanations are sleep inducers. Yawn! They involve an excessive amount discussion and literal adherence to a set of rules or laws, often to the detriment of understanding the underlying intent or spirit of those rules. This approach typically emphasizes external behaviors and regulations as the means to achieve salvation, spiritual growth, or approval, rather than focusing on genuine faith, inner transformation, or the principles behind the rules.

Key Characteristics of Legalistic Explanations

Focus on the Letter of the situation, not the Spirit. The letter is to the point while the spirit of the situation is a personal interpretation that might not be good enough. Legalistic Explanations place serious emphasis on the rules and regulations that address the situation. These are derived from the collective experience of people who resolve problems in this domain of problems. People who address Legalistic Explanations have learned to place heavy emphasis on the importance of following specific rules and details for each situation. This is this case even if it means that a Cybersecurity team may miss the bigger picture or the compassion behind the law. The point is that the Rules and Regulations emerge from experience with resolving issues involved in Legalistic Explanations.

- **Rules Over Relationship:** The relationship becomes secondary to the system of rules and regulations governing and directing it.
- **Fragments Emphasis on Earning vs. Success:** Behavior and good work are seen as a way to earn success or favor with management, rather than as a response to the Legalistic Guidelines.
- **Judgmental Attitudes:** A legalistic approach often breeds a critical or judgmental attitude toward others, viewing them as less capable or knowledgeable for not consistently following the Cybersecurity guidelines of the organization.
- **Personally Defined Cybersecurity Guidelines:** Legalism can involve the addition of employee define personal

opinions and regulations to the Cybersecurity procedures transforming them into Guidelines that are more opinionated than the original Cybersecurity Professional Practices and Guidelines.

Core Concepts in Theories of Explanation

Theories of Explanation are indeed surprising if not interesting. While the average person can explain Cybersecurity concepts in his or her sleep, this is not how we do it philosophically and scientifically to be more rigorous. The perspectives of Mother Philosophy and Rational and Empirical Science require:

- Deep Thought,
- Debate,
- Research,
- Sometimes Guesses,
- Argumentative Opinions, And
- Even Pre-Explanation Research.

In this view, explanations are more than ordinary opinions. However, for the general population, explanations often are little more than personal opinions. Formal Explanations consist four defining components as identified below:

- **Explanandum:** The phenomenon or statement that needs to be explained.
- **Explanans:** The set of sentences or facts that are used to account for the phenomenon.
- **Laws of Nature:** Principles or regularities that are essential to many scientific explanations, especially within the DN model.
- **Causation:** A central concept in causal accounts, with theories debating whether explanations should focus on the

existence of cause-and-effect relationships or more broadly on causal information.

Why These Theories Matter

They help distinguish between mere description and true explanation.

They provide frameworks for evaluating the quality and structure of scientific and ordinary explanations. They explore whether explanations are purely formal, causal, unifying, or context-dependent. The primary challenge of scientific explanation is determining what counts as a good explanation. This problem emerged from the limitations of early models, like the covering law model, which failed to capture explanatory asymmetry and allowed for irrelevant explanations. Subsequent theories developed by philosophers of science grappled with how to account for scientific explanations that involve unobservable entities, the relationship between explanation and causation, and the existence of non-causal forms of explanation, all of which present significant philosophical difficulties.

The Power and Force of Explanations in Human Activity Systems

Every human being is a member of a distinct Human Activity System. As a matter of fact, each person lives his or her life as a member of several Living Systems. A fundamental aspect of such participation is how each person navigates his or her life as members in these living Systems. At the center of their lives, regardless of whom they may be and how they may live their lives, are the daily explanations they receive and give in response to the situations they experience every single day of their lives.

Some of these explanations will be simple, but others will doubtlessly be complicated. This is because they will experience a wide range of explanations from the simple to the profound. These explanations will come to them as answers to a wide range of problems or as predictions of project outcomes. Answer will also come along in a form that further complicates troublesome situations. They may be seeking sets of true statements but they unfortunately receive probable predictions of outcomes. The explanations may be incomplete and fail to answer the questions they have continually asked. As you have seen so far in this book, explanations are amazing. Many different kinds of explanations can be given. Some of these will be helpful and some not. Whatever the case, we should never give up. To enjoy success in life, we need solid and relevant explanation. So, never give up. Keep it going forever forward. You will ultimately gain the most suitable explanation for your situation. Through explanation, your answers, predictions, statements, descriptions, and difficulties are all there. Never give up. Certainly, explanation have difficulties, but through knowledge and perseverance, you will gain the best possible explanation for your situation. Your menus of explanations will consist of the following table of possibilities:

- Explanations as answers
- Explanation as beyond descriptions
- Explanations as probable predictions
- Explanations as Sets of True Statements
- Explanations as involving Statements of what is to be explained
- Explanations and their difficulties
- Completeness of Explanations

Key Challenges of Finding Explanations

Believe it or not, but explanations can be difficult to organize and deliver. Who would thing that explanations would be a problem? Everyone has an explanation for you. You do not even have to ask. From Tom and Jerry to Mickey Mouse, everyone has explanations for everything. Ask Superman. If he is not around, ask the person on the street. They always have explanations. Or better yet, ask a politician. Politicians will always give you the explanation you want. Just ask them.

Explanations are Asymmetrical

When you get your explanation, remember "Buyer Beware". Make sure that you explanation is Asymmetrical. Just because Bill likes Helen, it does not mean that Helen likes Bill. Just because two Fords equal two cars this does not mean that two cars equal two Fords.

Relevancy is the Pavement of the Explanation Highway

Irrelevance is the sin of explanation, if you are offering an explanation to someone, never deliver irrelevant information. Everything should make logical sense. If a person jumps out of a plane without a parachute, do not blame that person's death on the lack of clouds in the sky. If the explanation is not relevant, it is of no use.

Historical Context

If you have decided to become a seriously reliable explainer, become a Philosopher of Science and study the deep history of the Theories of Explanation. There are a bunch of them or sure. If we go back in time to around the 1950s or 1960s, we will see that the concern with scientific explanation took a more serious direction with the contribution of Carl Hempel and his law mode. Although his work was noted, it had a few serious constraints with his insufficient concern for asymmetry and relevance. Eventually, philosophers developed causal and non-causal theories as alternatives.

Theories of Explanation

The interesting things about the Theories of Explanation is that they offer a mixed bag of interpretations that are often shaped by one theory of another. F or example, such a theory of explanation may deliver a detailed description of something that actually exists in external reality outside the human mind. This would take the form of a realist explanation, because it is really real outside the mind. On the other hand, an explanation may take the form of an explanation that serve a purpose that does not identify reality by rather describes, and even organize, a person's experience with a certain kind of reality that results from experiments, studies, and knowledge transfer without direct experience of the subject of the studies. This is the kind of explanation that is common in model-building exercises that facilitate projects. They are an exercise in logic rather than explanations of "what is".

For the realist, however, real processes, entities, and transformations are essential for resolving why an explanation is given. beyond realist and anti-realist explanations, another kind of explanation that is employed by some thinkers simply explains the way people deliver their explanations. These are the explanations of explanations, or the explanations^2. Considering the preceding, I suppose we can say that explanation enables communications among individuals that deepens understanding about the topics of explanation. Or is a purely intellectual, i.e., cognitive, activity that delivers a cognitive representation.

The Deeper Philosophical View of Explanation

Human beings generally live their lives by navigating their way through the explanations which influence the intensity, direction, thinking, opinions, and behaviors of their lives. This is because whatever explanations are, they are at the core of life and many of life's decisions. Explanations cause reactions and these reactions cause much of the stuff that defines each person's life. Many explanations are intended to inform decisions about actions to be taken that generally impact one's life as least a little or often a lot. Think about your own life. How have you generally reacted to the explanations you have received, either good or bad. Perhaps your reactions are only emotional. Your emotions are still a reaction.

However, honesty would compel us to admit that some explanations may have caused us to modify the direction of our lives. This direction could be just what we were looking for. Or, it could have been something that we would have preferred to avoid. Nevertheless, at the core of this situation was the explanation received. Lucky us! Apparently, the explanations in these cases were indeed causative. Aristotle would love it. Perhaps this is why many Philosophers, myself included, think of explanation as a causative agency. No kidding. Think about your life. Have explanation ever caused you to do something that you would not have done with the explanation you had received?

Occasionally, explanations ae quite powerful. Sometimes they are a waste of time. Nevertheless, explanations of even a single event or a specific situation, an authentic phenomenon of concern, often turns out to be the identification of a cause. Therefore, we say that when we explain an event or phenomenon, we are identifying the cause. For example, Ann says to Bill: "It sure is cold today, Bill. What on God' green earth happened out there!" Bill being an intelligent gentleman, something rare for him, explained: "Ann, the temperature dropped 45 degrees in an hour." So, Bill gave an explanation that at one level identified the cause of the situation which was "good enough" for Ann. "45 degrees, WOW! No wonder I am so cold. Thanks Bill.

If Ann was a philosopher or a scientist, Bill's answer would not do. This is because a scientist or philosopher would want a more informed explanation. For example, Bill would say that the speed of the molecules in the air slowed by 18% and the wind changes direction by 23% and increased in speed by 6.3 miles per hour. Ann would, of course reply, "Thanks Bill, that clears it up. Did the distance between the earth and the sun change at all? I realize that the moon is slowly moving away from earth. Does this influence our climate?" There are as many explanations being given here, and they implicitly focus on cause and effect. They are causal replies for sure. Aristotle is right again. It seems that every word does matter when we are trying hard to understand the nature of explanation and its link to causation. This does sound a lot like the Philosophy of Science.

Obviously, if Philosophers of Science have decided that the "Problem of Explanation" is worth their time and is worthy of pursuit, it must matter in some way to the non-philosophers among us. But, aren't we all really philosophers in some way? After all, everyone is curious about something in some way or other. Curiosity in one way or another is the beginning of philosophy. How, what, and why are great words for philosophers, but they do not own them. We all want to know How, What and Why about a lot of stuff. Now why is that? How can it possibly be true? What if it is not true? It makes me wonder: What is Truth? My gosh, I must be a philosopher.

Obviously, "The Problem of Explanation" is at the center of the discussion about Theory and the Reality of what is outside the mind, the phenomena of the world. This is so because our explanations could be erroneous but reality is really what it is when it is. When our explanations describe reality as it is in itself, our explanations have delivered truth when a one-to-one correspondence exists between reality and the explanation given about that reality. In some interesting way, you might say that we are explaining the causal structure of the world. If this is so, we should keep in mind that "Semantics Matter".

Have you ever noticed that when people ask you to explain something, the request can be quite irrational but with just a different word of two, it could become rational? This is important to note because sane people do not like to ask irrational questions unless they are playing a trick on someone. People are more interested in knowing the "why" of something rather than the "what" because it is the great objective of rational interest. Think about it. We have collected an impressive amount of knowledge that explains the "what" of it all. But, when we ask the why question, we quickly become disappointed. If you ae a scientist, you probably know what I mean. In science, we certainly want to know more than the what of things. For example, I know a lot about the what of the Cosmos, but I do not know much about the why of it all. For example, "Why" is there not nothing? Is not that a good question? If not, why? Oppenheim (1948) points out that description alone is never enough. For example, science is all about going below the surface to understand the why the what is the way it is. What do you think?

Do you know that people as a rule of life like good explanations? Of course, you probably do. Unless, of course, you are indifferent to explanation in general. There are plenty of people who do not want to be smarter. It takes focused effort. Intelligence, motivation, concentration, and desire are the prerequisites to mastering the Theory of Explanation. Many people do not even realize that a Theory of Explanation exists. It does and it can be theoretical complicated. It can even be difficult to explain. Imagine that! A Theory of Explanation that is difficult to explain. Who would ever have imagined such a thin? Today, Philosophers of Science study the Theory of Explanation from several perspectives including those listed here:

- Causal Realism,
- Constructive Empiricism,
- Ordinary Language Philosophy,
- Cognitive Science and
- Naturalism and Scientific Realism.

As reasoned by Michael Scriven (1959: p. 456), we do good when we remember that an explanation can occasionally be attributed as a cause. For Scriver, this capacity for identifying causes is:

- Learned,
- Better developed in some people than in others,
- Can be tested, and
- Is the basis for what we call judgments

Explanations Requires Explanation

It is a common experience for one person to ask another person to explain something. It could be an academic request, a work request, a personal request, a social request, and any one of many other possibilities. The request could be approached as a Metaphysical request, a Realist request, an Anti-Realist Request, and Epistemological Request, an uninformed request, a causal Request, a Logical Relationship Request, a Knowledge Seeking Request, a Deliberative Request, an Unconscious Request, a Propositional Request, an Instinctive Request, and so forth.

The Theory of Explanation has covered a lot of territory and has emerged in many forms from rule bearing and then on to spontaneously constitutional and even deeply neurological. Many thinkers have made their contributions to the problem of explanation. Can you explain that. Even the Philosopher, Psychologist, and the even Physical Scientist have made their contribution to the dialogue about the nature of Explanation. I am sure that you have your opinion. I know that I have several myself.

Theorists of Explanation

Over the years, many people have contributed to the Nature of Explanation dialogue. Much of it has not yet been resolved. For example, Wesley Salmon's causal theory of explanation is perhaps the most influential developed within the Realist Tradition. Also, van Fraassen's Theory reasons that explanation is a process of communication in a logical relationship between questions and answers. Departing from this, Achinstein actively characterizes explanation as the pursuit of understanding. He stipulated that all explanations are given relative to a set of instructions ultimately determined by the individual asking the question. This is interesting for sure. Obviously, there are so many people who have so many different views on the nature of an explanation that you have to be a deep thinker to know who to support. Although people are lost when it comes to explanation, we are making some progress little-by-little. Since, *"Studies in the Logic of Explanation,"* 1948 when Hempel and Oppenheim made their case about Explanation. There have indeed been many different perspectives about the nature of explanation and its influence in human affairs. Isn't that surprising? I always that explanation was merely a matter of clarifying a situation. I find it surprising that explanations can be explicitly propositional in nature, but it may also be unconscious, instinctive, and involve no explicit propositional knowledge what so ever. You do not have to know anything to explain something?

I would have never guessed. I need to find someone who can explain this to me. Perhaps it is actually a fundamentally neurological process through which explanatory understanding is understood by reference to activation patterns within a neural network. Patterns of activation> Wow, I hope they can explain this. I guess this I naturalistic in some way. It certainly undermines the idea that knowledge is prior to understanding. Do you understand that? Do not worry, you do not need any knowledge. Isn't life grand!

Generally, some people suggest that the idea, basically, is that explanation is not something that occurs on the basis of pre-confirmed truths. Rather, I can explain something without knowing anything about it. In this view, successful explanation is actually part of the process of confirmation itself. I know for sure that people have explained things to me without understanding anything at all about what they were telling me. They were simply repeating something they had earlier heard from someone else. They were simply repeating the unknown. I have worked with people who merely seek to attain "explanatory unification". Sounds good, doesn't it. They also seek "consilience" because good explanations necessarily tend to produce a more unified body of knowledge. Some people seek explanation to manipulate the three basic components of a world picture including: (a) observed objects and events; (b) unobserved objects and events, and (c) nomological connections, so as to achieve a maximum of "explanatory coherence."

Interestingly, over the years, many Philosophical Naturalists have embraced this idea of "inference to the best explanation" (IBE) as a fundamental principle of scientific reasoning. This means that theories are successful because they are "good enough" and they are "good enough" because they are approximately true. On the other hand, the Traditional Realists do not think of realism as a scientific hypothesis, but as an independent metaphysical dialogue.

This works for some people because every such IBE view stipulates, as a condition of having explanatory power at all, that a statement must be true or well-confirmed to possess explanatory power. This is especially the case when an explanation increases our understanding, not simply by being the correct answer to a particular question, but by increasing the coherence of our entire belief system.

This, then, would be a powerful explanation. Whatever we do with explanation, we do well to never forget that "inference to the best explanation" really can only mean "inference to the best explanation given to date." Time can correct what we think we know today. None of us yet know the very best explanation for anything. Brilliant people exist. They would be the first to tell you that they have not yest crafted the best possible explanation for their area of interest. They may have great explanations. They may have the explanations that everyone deeply loves. Nevertheless, these two conditions may not yet be the best. We do not know yet. There are still a large number of disagreements about what explanations are and which specific explanation is the best ever, forever.

I say this because there still are a number of metaphysical disagreements. For example, Realists and Anti-Realists disagree about the kinds of Ontological commitments one actually makes when one accepts an explanation. Beyond this, there are also a number of unresolve Meta-Philosophical disagreements that seem permanent. In this case, Naturalists and non-Naturalists continually disagree about the relevance of Scientific Inquiry to a broadly philosophical theory of explanation. These disputes are not about to be resolved in a very long time without an important philosophical insight. We certainly need someone who can deliver a targeted problem-solving environment to address these outstanding philosophy issues.

Cognitive Tour

A Problem-Solving Environment is much more than a web page. It is an environment of knowledge, expertise, and the insights gained from successful global experience developed by solving a wide range of hard and soft problems throughout the world in Rapid Real Time, that's "RRT". I thought I had mastered this 15 years ago but it took me more than half a Century to develop the skills and experience required to ignite that 15 years of deep focus and hard work on an understanding of Explanations. My success in these challenges did not take years to earn. They took many life- times to nurture, design, and launch. I still remember some of those people. Some of them were simply brilliant. I enjoyed knowing them and learning from them. While smart people learn from each other, the not so smart people learn from no one. I have known plenty of those also. Personally, I prefer the smart people. Learning never stops. So now let's get to the central issues in this book series, Insider Threat Prevention, an old but also new kind of challenge because of the rapid developments in Information Systems and associated technologies. Who can you trust with your organization's most vital, valuable, and confidential information?

7: Insider Threat Prevention and the Challenge of Explanation

To Ignore the Psychological is a Formula for Failure.

What is an Insider Threat? People tell me that an Insider Threat is a person with a bad attitude who holds a grudge and thus seeks to damage the existing cyber environment of an organization in one or more ways. WOW! This says a lot but leaves out even more than it says. This answer is really too general don't you think? "Bad Attitude" in what way and how deep and how enduring and for what reason and how strong and how long and how this and that? Please Explain. There are people who display simply wonderfully good attitudes who will steal your vital data for a price. This person could even be an SVP or even a trusted consultant. How do you know who to trust? Of course, this is the wrong question. Personally, I never much like the Trust word for a number of reasons. I like delivery and performance better.

Remember the TV show in the 50s, *Who Do You Trust,* running from *1956* to 1963? It was entertaining and educational. The modern version is a challenge. It can quickly put a company out of business overnight. Johnny Carson went on to enjoy a long and prosperous career. Hopefully the Insider Threats do not. Today, Insider Threats are both people and systems. It is indeed very complicated. Fundamentally, to prevent Insider Threats today an organization requires an abundance of standards and procedures and associated prevention programs and focused technologies and protocols and insightful people. In other words, organizations need to be designed or redesigned to enable a rigorous environment of Insider Threat Prevention. Considering all of the above, let's take a deeper look at Insider Threat Prevention.

Insider Threats Do Not Emerge Only from the Inside

Insider Threat Prevention, and Mitigation when Prevention fails, has certainly seized "Front Stage" since the emergence of fast networks, globally Integrated Information Systems (ISS) and electronic social networks. Today people see Cybersecurity as a Never-Ending challenge. Obviously, cybersecurity is here to stay. Executives would not be able to get to sleep at night without the confidence it delivers. On the surface, this seems plausible, and executives get their sleep. But, should they be so much asleep? **Oremus!** Let us take a look. I understand that the average cost per Cyber-attack is approximately $220,000. It could be higher or lower depending on the day of the week and the time of the day. All I can say for sure is that this is a painful cost. We all know this. What can we do about it. Well, let me think about it for a minute.

OK, I thought about it. The solution, obviously, is a design solution, not only a technical solution. We have to change how we look at organizations, their design, and their evolutionary management. It is long past time to do this. After all, organization, whether small or gigantic are indeed Human Activity Systems, or HAS, and they function as Evolutionary Guidance Systems, or EGS. Are you familiar with these?

Commonly I am told that people concerned about Cybersecurity and Insider Threat Mitigation spend much of their time designing and initiating Insider Threat Mitigation organizations and programs. Wouldn't it just be hunky-dory if we were so good at Insider Threat PREVENTION that mitigation would only be an afterthought because it would rarely be required? One can dream right? No, we can do more than dream. We can make it so. Captain Jean-Luc Picard would love it. So, let's take a closer look and start with where things are today as expressed in current thinking and see what could be different, that is, see where change for the better is possible. You will see that we can do more than hope and jump in and follow everyone else with our fingers crossed. We can actually do better. So, let's roll-up our sleeves and become the Positive Change Agents we have the power to be. I would like to begin by saying something about who the Insider Threats actually are. Sure enough, some of the culprits are indeed well-known, but many are not. Surprise, surprise.

Insider Threat Agents

Insider Threats Agents obviously come from within the organization. The Insider could be an executive, manager, an employee not in the management ranks. The Insider could be a full-timer or even a part-timer. He or she could even be an opportunistic visitor looking to make a "back-room" deal. It happens. Theoretically, this person could be anyone. Practically speaking, however, this person is rarely just anyone. Whoever this person happens to be, he or she has an agenda, hidden or otherwise.

Additionally, we have the visitors, regular or otherwise, known or unknown. This is someone who knows his or her way around socially, politically, and even formally. This is a person who enjoys a consultative or even a personal relationship with someone in a vulnerable position. Such visitors, or former employees, know their way around the environment of vulnerabilities. Such people enjoy deep organizational and institutional knowledge which grants them authorized access to places they should not go. But it happens and we need to protect the enterprise, and each other, against the unforeseen cybersecurity surprises that can eventually occur because of these unguarded moments.

Remember, it is not only about access to the data and systems, it is also about unforeseen damage to the hardware in unexpected places. Theft can also become the problem. Highly confidential business and management records can also become at risk. There is always an illegal market for something. Damage does not have to be done to the systems and data. Theft can also be a problem with the future plans of changes to the infrastructure being at risk. Some competitors like to know what each other are planning. So, today everything is a target. Even confidential information held by employees. We are speaking here of networks, Information Systems, data, and valuable assets even your corporate-wide HR-Personnel files. A Cyberterrorist can be extremely dangerous. Enter corporations have been put out of business because of Cyberterrorism. So, we should never take them lightly. Some of the current defensive strategies have succeeded in defending the organization that have adequately employed them. Indeed, they are quite promising for some organizations. However, we need a Cyber Security Program that works for everyone, is easier to understand, and is cost effective, that is, financially affordable. Since so many different Cyber-terrorists are out there using different tactics and attack strategies, our defensive posture must be meta-methodological. This is a systems design thing.

Since people tell me that the cyber-criminal could be anyone, obviously, if this is true, we need an approach that protects the entire organization without confusing people with a complexity that will eventually be simplified by the cyber-criminal. Realistically, however, it is only a theory that the cyber-criminal could be anyone. I guess that I should mention that it is a theory I do not support for obvious reasons. Not everyone is corrupt. Not everyone has a criminal personality. Not everyone is dishonest. Indeed, many people enjoy a well-formed and strong moral foundation and ethical code of conduct. Indeed, their morals, and ethics are well-developed, strong, and sincere. Their character is not for sale.

Although it is quite true that Insiders have indeed compromised sensitive information, damaged team reputations, caused lost revenue, stolen intellectual property, reduced market share of companies, and even harmed workmates, these were a relatively small number of people who manipulated their workmates or friends. For these morally challenged people, it was all in the timing and the perfection of their well-hidden covert insincerity. Sadly, it only takes one of these kinds of people to ignite disaster in a company. Many of these people fail for a number of reasons. When they succeed, however, the damage they cause may overwhelm everyone on the receiving end of the tragedy. While it is true that some organizations had to pay a high ransom to recover from their Cyber-attacks, other organizations had to shut down all their business operations and completely walk away because their ransom and restart costs were so prohibitive.

Cyber-Terror is indeed a very dangerous, expensive, and disruptive assault on any organization. This is not a secret. For many executives and governments, it is a clearly recognized expensive discomfort. Nevertheless, Cyber-Terror can still be defeated. In the final analysis, the ultimate solution will be a trip down memory lane. Believe it or not! For many people, it will be less obvious but more stringent and secure than the currently recommended approaches followed by many organizations around the globe. Insider Threat Mitigation has enjoyed a very, very significant amount of attention. Many solutions have been delivered. Nevertheless, the attacks are increasing at an increasing rate.

Developing Effective Insider Threat Programs

To be blunt, Cyber-threats are no laughing matter. Let me repeat: They are increasingly complicated and more rapidly negatively impact an organization's many dimensions. The concepts and responses required to terminate the many Cyber-Threats that are out there today are demanding, expensive, and complicated. It can take great skill simply to neutralize these Cybersecurity threats. Nevertheless, the essence of the times we live in propels us to design and implement rigorous Cyber Security protections. By now, probably everyone understands that to mitigate both physical and cybersecurity threats, it is important to understand the risks posed by insiders and then build a comprehensive Insider Threat Mitigation Program that addresses the operational, legal, and regulatory threats faced daily by organizations.

Beyond this, however, we are wise to also consider the disruptions that potentially can be caused by the people we trust who unintentionally, and possibly intentionally (people change you know), engage in bad acts throughout the organization and across all systems throughout the company and perhaps even beyond. The most common response to this Insider Threat Scenario is the initiation of several well thought out projects to design and implement a seriously proactive two-part program that focuses first on Threat Prevention and then secondly on Threat Mitigation. This is the common management plan to ensure Cyber-Security resilience. The commonly recognized plan goes something like this:

- Form expert working group;
- Organize responsibilities for each member of the group;
- Define specific Insider Threats unique to the specific environment;
- Identify common Insider Threats common among environment in general;
- Develop capabilities to engage ITP processes;
- Develop capabilities to engage IPM processes;
- Detect and identify all threats;
- Assess Threats risks, and
- Manage each risk before concerning behaviors manifest in an actual insider incident.
- Engage in continuous cost versus benefits analysis

An effectively designed and managed ITP program will do much of value for an ITP team and the entire organization, including the following:

- Protect critical assets;

- Deter violence and carelessness;
- Eliminate unintentional incidents;
- Assure Revenue flows;
- Prevent and/or reduce revenue loss
- Secure intellectual property;
- Prevent the compromise of sensitive and proprietary data;
- Protect good name of the organization;
- Eliminate internal and external thefts of proprietary technologies and information.

Since this is an important ITP issues, let me repeat: Insider Threats may generate losses through:

- Infrastructure damage;
- Reduction of productivity;
- Theft or violation of intellectual property;
- Damaging exposure of highly valuable proprietary and sensitive data, and
- Assault on the reputation of the enterprise.

ITP and the Possibility of Unplanned Costs

In the cosmos of Cyber Crime, Insider Threats present the daunting threat of critical costs overruns that could defeat the entire enterprise and lead to its closing. This is especially the case for medium to smaller companies. This is so because of the expanse of the Insider Threats. Many of these threats are well known and have a history of including the following:

- Personal Injury
- Theft of Proprietary Intellectual Property
- Financial Loss
- Privacy Loss

- Disruptions of all Information Technology Services
- Unauthorized Disclosure
- Infrastructure Damage
- Loss of Life of employee or visitor as an involved person

Obviously, with so much at risk and even more riding on the outcome of resilient Insider Threat Prevention and Insider Threat Mitigation programs, Research and Development, Planning and Design, Implementation and Post-Implementation reviews and testing are very much common sense. Is some way, we are going back to the beginning of computer programming and Information Systems Design, and taking these skills to their ultimate levels of Cyber Security capability. We will review such a project by going back to review the critical terms of Cyber Security Project Management that can make or break any Cyber Security program.

Truth be told, Insider Threat Prevention is not a walk in the park, but if we do this effectively, we need to spend less time on Insider Threat Mitigation. This makes sense don't you think? Let's do the tour now and highlight some of the concepts of ITP that are essential for mastering Cyber Security. Let me start by asking you: How do you define and describe Insider Threat Prevention? I do not mean Mitigation.

Effective Insider Threat Prevention

Let's begin here by defining Insider Threat Prevention. There are many people who are "Insiders" but never think about it. So, I will clear it up here. It should be obvious, but confusion remains. Even some employees do not think of themselves as Insiders. The typical definition contains the following information: An insider is:

- Any person **who has** authorized access to an organization's resources including personnel, facilities, information, equipment, networks, and systems
- Any person **who has** authorize knowledge of an

organization's resources including personnel, facilities, information, equipment, networks, and systems

- Any person **who previously had** authorized access to an organization's resources including personnel, facilities, information, equipment, networks, and systems
- Any person **who previously had** authorized knowledge of an organization's resources including personnel, facilities, information, equipment, networks, and systems

First Consideration

This is a very detailed and somewhat repetitive list, but I want to be as comprehensive as possible because the topic is so serious. Do you see anything wrong with this very detailed list? We are not finished yet, but the question is valid. This definition states that an "Insider" is someone with "authorization". What about the unauthorized people who over time have managed to collect vital info because of the carelessness of the Insiders?

Some of these "outsiders" have collected and gathered more information than that possessed by the Authorized Insiders. They may not be Authorized Insiders, but they may be even more of a Threat than the Authorized Insiders, or they would not be collecting everything they can about the organization's personnel, facilities, information, equipment, networks, and systems. However, certain people indeed do exactly this. It is time to ask the important question here: How do organizations protect themselves from these unauthorized Insiders? Why are they collecting the information they are managing to collect through the carelessness of the authorized Insiders? What is their plan? What is their goal? What are the possible outcomes? How often have trusted Insiders disappointed you or someone in your organization? How was it managed? How badly did it damage the organization? What did you learn from it that will assist you with managing your Cybersecurity Program and the people working on it?

Welcome to my world. I am not an overnight success.
- Ray Newkirk

Second Consideration

This is a person who, for some reason, is "trusted" by someone important in the organization. Welcome to the Boy Scouts of America where Trust is so central to everything they do, and eve that was violated. These "trusted persons will often have gained access to important sensitive information from employees including special purpose organization members, and special project participants and team members. How do you ensure confidentiality is maintained in these situations? Is it through signed contracts and personal assurances?

Third Consideration

This is a person who is in possession of a special badge or controlled access device that identifies him or her as a vendor, repair person, contractor, consultant, person with a computer for problem solving, service technician, janitor, and even a person from a Cyber Security organization. Some of these people may enjoy access to the company's private network. This is a rare situation, but it happens, especially with start-ups. This situation may also involve special contractors who have in-depth knowledge about an organization's pricing and cost structure, products and services, plans and forecasts. This may even include the costs of business operations associated with a long list of its strengths and weaknesses.

These "external-Insiders" may even know what products and services are the most valuable to an organization and even how to alter the numbers.

Think about the hidden implications here in this Third Consideration. There is so much that can go wrong in this Age of Cybersecurity. No wonder so many influential Leadership "experts" speak so much about the need to develop trust throughout the enterprise. It is kind of like being a missionary in an organization. I think there is a better way. I like to see performance as a measure of confidence with Insiders, whoever they are. Judas was a real person. An organization can have confidence in an employee's ability to deliver great performance because that employee consistently does so. However, this does not mean that particular employee is completely trustworthy all the time. I am sure that you get the point here. Always be careful with trust. In today's high-tech & A/I unfolding world, be supremely careful about who you trust, how long you will need to trust them, and what you will trust them with. Even Boy Scout Leaders sometimes go bad.

Fourth Consideration

If you an executive in a Leadership role, here are a few ideas worth considering about your people and the Threat of Cybersecurity. There are Insiders and Outsiders who think and behave as if they are Insiders. They are people who have attained in-depth knowledge about an organization's confidential Business Strategies, Goals, and Execution Plans. Moreover, they have enjoyed access to important plans for the future that identify projects to be launched to increase the short-term revenues and then leverage these to launch the projects that will build revenues enough to enhance the Cybersecurity Program in a way that will enable the company to increase market share and add Cybersecurity staff to secure the company as it grows.

Fifth Consideration

In the first Four considerations above, I have discussed Cybersecurity from the business enterprise perspective. In this respect, I introduced a few fundamental challenges which everyone in business now faces as a basic Cybersecurity obligation. When we move this concern from business to the Government and think about more than business Cybersecurity alone, the context of government services and operations magnifies the seriousness of implementing an in-depth Cybersecurity Program. Just imagine the risk here in managing government Cybersecurity. A single individual with access to Government Cybersecurity processes could initiate a disaster on the first attempt. Obviously, a single person with access to protected Governmental information, could cause damage to national security and public safety on a large scale. Such a Cybersecurity event could even impact foreign operations. Failed Cybersecurity would be a disaster.

Take a Deep Breath

Obviously, we have plenty to do to produce and implement a robust and effective Cybersecurity Program in our businesses and agencies. Much work remains to be done, even for those organizations who have done plenty of ITP work already. Whatever you do, it is never enough. The question about whether a person is an Insider or Outsider Threat is most often a nonsensical one because the outsiders have generally gained access equal to or better than many insiders. Experience tells us that before Insiders became Insider Threats, they were like every other employee in the organization. Whenever an Insider hits a very personal inflection point everything begins to change. A transformation occurs and, "Bingo", the Inside is now an Insider Threat.

The question, of course, is what ignited this transformation from just an Insider to an Insider Threat? Generally, the progression from trusted insider to insider threat occurs because of just the right mix of stressors, personal predispositions, and formative behaviors. In other words, just the right mix of psychological and behavioral factors. If we identify the factors early enough, they will be helpful to us in identifying the Insider and heading off the Insider's now malicious act of behavior. As these people went from good to bad, some of them become very proficient at developing their threat agendas. It is time to take a deep breath and then press on. We are getting close, but no Home-Run yet. We have not arrived at a place where it makes sense to check out the list of activities involved in executing a Cybersecurity Plan of Action:

- Define Insider Threat for Your Organization's Specific Environment
- Define Your Cybersecurity Best Practices Specific to Your Organization
- Define Cybersecurity Training & Development Confidentiality Guidelines Governing Highly Confidential Internal Cybersecurity Approaches and Techniques
- Establish Your Cybersecurity Continuous Training & Development Program
- Define Unintentional Insider Threats
- Identify the Types of Unintentional Insider Threats
- Define Intentional Insider Threats
- Identify the Types of Intentional Insider Threats
- Define Third Party Threats
- Define Collusive Threats
- Determine the Range of Expressions of Threat Reactions
- Identify Possible Expressions of Insider Threats
- Determine organization-wide expectations for the Cybersecurity program.
- Convey the expectations tom associated managers effectively.
- Create an appropriately suited, protective, and supportive cybersecurity culture.

Keys for Success in ITP and ITM

- Know Your People
- Establish the Proven Operational Approach

- Detect
- Identify
- Assess
- Manage

Forming a Safe Environment to Overcome the Insider Threat

Combining cultural and systemic actions will fulfill eight core functions as listed below:

1. Establish a safe environment to prevent Insider Violence and other hostile acts.
2. Maintain a safe environment to prevent Insider Violence and other hostile acts.
3. Take Appropriate Actions to Stop Insider Threats form succeeding.
4. Institute the appropriate Guidelines and Controls to block Insider Threat Actors from engaging the actions.
5. Continuously Monitor and Detect al threatening Insider Threats or other concerning behaviors.
6. Design and apply methodology to consistently identify individuals at risk of becoming an Insider Threats.
7. Design and apply process to develop information about both the actual and potential insider threats.
8. Resolve potential and actual insider threats before they escalate to violence, espionage, sabotage, or theft.

Some Valuable Points Worth Remembering

From a national perspective, Insider Threats are a pain even for the people who wish harm on all of u. Strange enough some of them probably work for us. Probably. Insider Threats are everywhere. Isn't this a real downer! We know what they know and they know what we know, mostly. The game is afoot Watson. It's like drinking water.

Everyone drinks water by drinking water. The containers and temperatures change but the is H^2O is still H^2O, and everybody drinks it.

Insider Threats are wide ranging and inconsistent. The targets of a Cybersecurity Threat are whatever can be damaged. This includes nearly everything including the mission of the organization, data, Information Systems, products, facilities, equipment, people, networks, finances, resources, and even the hopes and dreams of the executive staff. If the Insider can do the damage, the insider will do it without ever looking back. It couldn't happen to a nicer company. It is interesting to note that throughout the Cyberattack, the Insider Threat Actor will have previously enjoyed enough trust by the right people within the organization to form a trusting relationship that made the attack possible.

Each Insider Threat Actor will have currently enjoyed or have previously experienced a good enough trusting relationship with their victim to be able to act in a way that is outside the expectations of that probably well-established and trusting relationship. Obviously, this is evidence that organizations do well to tailor their approach to the Insider Threat situation to protect the unique nature of their operating environment and what they value. This is especially the case since Insider Threats are mostly intentional and only sometimes unintentional. A significant portion of Insider Threats involve negligent or accidental behaviors. What management does well to remember is that the Threat will do its damage in various ways depending on the nature of the organization, the type of work done or sector within the organization, the products produced, services performed, and the assets that should be protected from utter destruction.

I should remind everyone that Insider Threats are complicated. Sometimes it seems that with Insider Threat 1+1 = 276. Really. No kidding. This is because some intentional Insider Threats are actually not malicious. Believe It or not. I am not sure that I believe it yet. Not malicious? Actually, this makes some sense, but poor math. Obviously, an inside threat malicious actor does a large number of malicious acts without every intending to do any harm to an organization or an individual within that organization. I have known several of these people. They merely wanted to destroy a few of their organization's databases but they did not have any ill will for any of the people there. They were indeed friendly criminals bent on destroying the systems there while not hurting anyone there. Go figure. Ouch! Ignorance like that is indeed painful to confront. This is when you have to say: "Pardon me, sir. I do not wish to ruin your day, but you are under arrest. You have the right to remain silent..."

It is true, when it comes to Cybersecurity, people are a double-edged sword. While people are the strongest link of a Cybersecurity Program, we are also the weakest link. Our organizations are vulnerable to Cyber-crime because we, the people, are the deepest and widest vulnerability. We require threat-free access to systems, databases, Intellectual property, data, facilities, resources, and also most importantly, colleagues, managers, and workmates we cannot function much or very well. Insider Threats, and all that this means, reduces or even eliminates personal and team safety, reduces product and business value, and seriously damages operations. Obviously, following the right Principles and Guidelines is essential more than ever.

Some Important Principles and Guidelines

Insider Threat Prevention is all about preventing Insider Threats from emerging and when they do from succeeding. I have listed some commonly accepted principles and guidelines below:

- A potent ITP Security Programs is holistic. It does not overlook any security strategy but includes the most adaptive, responsive, and reliable.
- People are at the center of ITP security and then systems

because people design the systems of ITP Security.

- If you use A/I to support ITP security, be careful. Advanced A/I may turn against you.
- Never overlook strong physical security as a component of ITP security. But understand what physical security includes.
- All ITP security stands on solid and rigorous information-centric principles of in-depth security processes.
- ITP security begins and ends with personnel assurance because ITP is about ensuring that people can do the right thing and assuring that they do.
- A successful ITP culture is enterprise-wide, never only local. Each company employee participates in ITP full time. No vacation from ITP is possible.
- ITP is continually evolving and adapting in response to a constantly emerging threat and response environment.

Over time people change. Some people transform their attitudes and become excellent employees and other people also transform their attitudes and become Insider Threats. What do you prefer? In such situations, managers and team members do well to understand, track and continually track the Insider Threat's interactions within the organization. In this respect, its kind of like being back in school when we had to be attentive to the Hall Monitors and follow their guidance. The more things change, the more they stay the same. "Forever Young" is right but the stakes have changed significantly. In the contemporary workplace, we ae expected to assert ourselves and get involved when we think that a workmate's behavior poses a threat to the organization.

If we notice that someone has begun to become an Insider Threat, we engage the Insider Threat Mitigation process. In this case, we openly promote and build a protective and supportive Cybersecurity culture everywhere possible within the organization. We do this to assist our colleagues with protecting corporate data, information, systems, and the core business valuables. As we do this, we also protect the privacy right and personal liberties of oneself and colleagues and other workmates. The key concerns here, of course, in cases like this include the expected behaviors of colleagues to ensure their safety as well as the security of company assets to assure their integrity. An adequate Insider Threat Mitigation Program has many concerns. Cybersecurity teams track several lines of interest including the following:

- The significance of employee behaviors and how they differ depending on the role or and responsibilities of individuals and teams in the organization;
- The expected behaviors and professional performance of vendors, contractors, consultants, and other visitors when they are either physically or virtually engaged with the organization to ensure deep security, and.
- The behaviors expected from partners or suppliers when handling or accessing organizational information or equipment to protect them from compromise to ensure that there is no compromise on security.

Generally, Insider Threat Mitigation programs deliver insights into sensitive and very confidential information about the behavior of employees of a target company or other organization. The problem here, of course, is one of balance between maintaining confidentially of critical information and the depth of transparency available. The problem of balancing authority, asset protection, privacy, transparency, and continual monitory is a difficult one, but must be done carefully.

Cybersecurity poses a difficult challenge for executives and their mangers, and indeed, throughout their entire organizations. Insider Threats are not new, but with the emergence of global networks Cybersecurity has become a very serious Threat Management challenge. The problem here, of course, is that the bad guys can anticipate what the good guys will do to defeat them and thus have a counter-attack ready to defeat our counter-attack. And so. it goes. WE have to get ahead of the bad guys and preserve our position of security.

Establishing a Culture of Insider Threat Prevention

Not everyone can lead an ITP or ITM Program. Such a leader would do well to excel in resilience, strategy, team building, and foresight. Ensuring that the right people are adequately educated about the dynamics of Insider Threat Prevention and ITM is critical to establishing a culture of reporting. Everything starts with targeted communications that lays the foundation for the future of the two kinds of Insider Threats resolutions. For the good of all the employees, and of course the company, these efforts absolutely become robust programs that can address many roadblocks and detours. Such is the nature of Cybersecurity defensive programs. No one gets a pass. No one gets a "get out of jail" card. No one gets a "Pass Go" and collect your bonus kind of thing. In the world of Cybersecurity, only one thing matters. It is a single word. This word has seven letters. This word starts with a capital "S". This word ends with a capital "S". It is a word everyone treasures. It is a word that every seeks. Unfortunately, it is a word that pits the Cybersecurity team members against the Cybersecurity "CRIMINAL INTRUDERS".

This single word that is so valuable, so crucial, so necessary consists of only seven letters. This single and simple word, respected by hero and criminal alike, and seriously desire by both parts of the human equation is: S-U-C-C-E-S-S. Yes, it is this word fit for even children but bitterly chased by conscience disabled fiends. I did not say friends.

Yes, Cybersecurity criminals are fiends in motion who would destroy countless lives without a single tear-drop if they could get their treasure: the trade secret, the highly confidential Intellectual Property, the new technology, the new proprietary systems design, the new formula, the valuable competitive information, and on and on and on. It never stops, and so very much can be at stake with each instant of an

Insider Cybersecurity violation, and so often much is at stake. Ask the people who lost their jobs. Ask the people who lost their companies. Ask the people who lost their investments. Ask the people who carry the scars of Cybersecurity failure on their minds. You probably pass a few of them each and every day without knowing their stories.

Work hard to ensure that this does not become your story. Life is full of ups and downs and surprises around every corner. Make your surprises happy ones full of love and celebrations of kindness and successes that you worked hard and studied diligently to achieve and share with family and friends throughout your lives. You can "MAKE IT SO" says Jean-Luc Picard. He is probably correct if he was talking about Cybersecurity Threat Prevention.

You see, Cybersecurity is an experience where people can guess what's going on quickly. This is because so many employees are in the P perfect Place for gaining a bit of knowledge, and definitely some valuable insight, about something going on in specific areas of the organization that is not acceptable with management. I have been told that many people have at least a bit of knowledge that Insider generated cybersecurity violations are in progress when they are actually in progress. It seems that Insiders do not do a good job of concealing their intentions to engage in a Cybersecurity attack again the organization in some way. It appears that the detection of threats is not much of a challenge because the intentions of the Cybersecurity criminal are generally obvious to a number of people within the organization from the very beginning of the threat. The problem here for employees is that they do not know whom to go to with their information about the Insider Threat in progress. Wow!

Employees do not know where to go or whom to go to with the Cybersecurity Threat information they have uncovered. Can you imagine! In this day and age, with Cybersecurity Threats increasing every month, and with cyber terrorists on the rampage, and most people not knowing where to go with the information about it. Thus,

Insider Threat Prevention fails once again. Commonly, Management and Executive Leadership deliver an inadequate organization-wide response to the perceived Cybersecurity violations that ignites damage throughout the organization. Such a cybersecurity attack can return an organization back to the Dark Ages. In cases such as these, management is forced to focus its attention on a wide range of Legal matters.

Cybersecurity and the LAW

Obviously, all laws and regulations have to be followed and actively monitored. The organization must be actively managed at all times to overcome the Insider Threat situation. Moreover, at the most fundamental level possible, Cybersecurity involves a significant number of legal concerns. These include concerns about the following:

- Privacy
- Civil Liberties
- Civil Rights
- Whistleblower Protection
- Health Privacy
- Educational Privacy
- Employment
- Liability
- Management
- Individual Due Process
- Criminal Penalties
- Safety Regulations

Effective Insider Threat Mitigation Programs

Legal is no joke. If management executes its duties adequately and Leadership fulfills its mandate to overcome every instance of Insider attack, the company will effectively neutralize the criminal insider. Management's task moving forward will be to design its Insider Threat Elimination Program to safeguard its unique:

- organization mission,
- culture,
- critical assets, and
- threat landscape.

The People Are Not Expendable Because They Matter

An organization's workforce can be attentive and actively care about defeating any instant of a Cyber Attack. They care about the organization and its people. On the other hand, a workforce can be indifferent, inattentive, insecure, and insincere about doing a good and professional job. Executive Leadership and management have much to do with attitudes like these. It is not all on the backs of the employees who work for them.

Many people do not want to go to work more than you might imagine simple because they very much dislike the people they report to and follow every single day in and day out. In time, their dislike for their bosses cripples their attitudes so much so that their good will becomes painfully neutralized, and very difficult to find again. For these employees, the Insider Threats they are concerned about are their workmates. In workplaces like this, everyone is rooting for the Cybercriminal, believe it or not. These kinds of workplaces are more common than you would ever think. Executives in terrible pits like these often blame their employees for such attitudes. They argue that responsible grown-ups would be bigger than this. They would not become part of the problem but would show their personal character by overcoming all obstacles and neutralize the Cyber Terrorists. This is what a grown-up would do. Not many people on Planet Earth would ever build a positive culture of "reporting and prevention" because they are not dishonest with their colleagues or themselves. For them to form a positive culture that actively defeats Cybersecurity attacks, meaning forming a culture of consistently reporting and preventing Insider attacks, such an organization would have to invest in the well-being of its employees to develop their resilience and

Cybersecurity effectiveness. If effort to realize such a transformation in employee attitudes is to happen, the organization would have to successfully complete the following four-part program:

1. Master and employ multi-disciplinary capabilities enabled by both specialized technologies and dedicated employee that can leverage the following:

- Organization type
- Organization size
- Team culture
- Nature of Business
- Malicious and Negligent Disposition of Insiders
- Value of business and
- Risk tolerance of business to acts of seriously dedicated Insider Threats.

1. Excel at applying the customary framework of detect & identify, assess, & manage for the prevention of, protection against, and mitigation of insider threats.
2. Establish a rigorous Cybersecurity culture that ensure civil liberties, while maintaining confidentiality in special circumstances.
3. Guide organizations in providing a responsive and mature environment in which threatening people, and other negative insiders, are identified and assisted to cooperate positively with the organization in its Cybersecurity protection plan.

Insider Threat Mitigation

Insider Threat Prevention is one of the enduring challenges we are forced to suffer through these days. This is because the very existence of Insider Theat Prevention alone is enough to expand the Threat Environment that is continually emerging throughout the world in diverse environment from business and military to even Research & Development environments everywhere. In fact, ITP can stir things up enough that Insider Threat Mitigation becomes essential to the success of a company even though it demands a serious commitment from senior management simply to get it operational.

Building and maintaining an Insider Threat Mitigation (ITM) Program demands well thought out processes, especially those listed below:

ITM Conceptualization

ITM Planning

ITM Oversight

ITM Remediation

Insider Threat Mitigation programs are multidisciplinary. They have to be because they cover so much behavioral territory. Anything can happen with some of these perpetrators. They offer bribes, blackmail, and battery. Since that can destroy core business functions and core Information Repositories as well as enterprise-wide Information Systems, they pose a significant threat to any business enterprise and government agency, and beyond. As you can see, Insider Threat Prevention is a critical strategy in minimizing the complexity of Insider Threat Mitigation.

As you can guess, just like ITP, Insider Threat Mitigation cries out for executive level sponsorship. Such commitment if an organization wishes to enhance its capacity and capability to dominate the Insider Threat of theft, localized damage and perhaps even enterprise-wide destruction. It has happened, and it can happen again. Those who take Insider Threat lightly possess a light-weight mind and need to move on. Practically speaking, a solid ITM Program simply extends and deepens existing safety and security program that exist to protect employees, systems, and products. Every company, even two person businesses, do well to possess crime and violence prevention policies, strategies, and guidelines with emergency notification protocols. I have seen one person businesses that actually have some of this in place to protect themselves. Imagine that. So, for these organizations, and people, a solid ITM Program can expand, adapt, and employ their existing guidelines as a foundation or perhaps framework for building a serious ITM Program. Why not?

For a small business, it is a time-consuming thing for sure. But such a project can go quickly once it gets started. A little bit of research, a business can purchase some recommended Guidelines to produce what is essential. Focus on the key principles of ITM, the Best Practices, along with the tools & techniques that are a must. Master the concepts of ITM. The point here is that you need to know what to do if you ever need what to do for ITM. The National Insider Threat Task Force (NITTF) offers some fine guidance to assist federal agencies with developing their Insider Threat Management programs. Although it is intended for Federal Agencies, it delivers some great guidance.

The NITTF created a list of guidelines for federal agencies and departments to assist them with developing their Insider Threat Management programs. This guidance shares some sound insights about several areas of ITP & ITM interest. For example, to establish an Insider Threat Program:

- Designate a Senior Official
- Form an Insider Threat Working Group
- Establish Governance and Publish Insider Threat Policy
- Implement a Formal Training and awareness program
- Create an Insider Threat Program Office
- Plan Senior Executive Engagement

- Determine the Best Fit
- Determine Program Ownership
- Determine What it Means to be the Responsible and Accountable Senior Official
- Functionally Describe an Insider Threat

The Simplicity of Explanations

I imagine that many people have never thought much about the deeper reality of explanations. Bill, explain this if you don't mind. Oh, sorry Bill. Helen, explain that if you have time. My gosh, won't anybody explain it to me? We've got to stop all the Cybersecurity violations before they become a threat to the survival of our business. Patricia, please explain it to them. It's simple Patricia, right? Right Ray, we have to hurry because the enable modulator is dissipating at 3^{10} X 1556 – 36^3+ 4200÷42^{13}+16 = 37-3 to infinity. Got it? We need to reduce this by 17% by noon today. Clear.

Well thanks Patricia. I knew I could count on you to explain the situation. I am sure everyone here feels better by now. Thanks. What, where did everybody go? Patricia it is simply amazing the impression you make on the team with your explanations. Everybody, and I do mean everybody, is continually talking about how amazed they are with your right to the point explanations. Great job Patricia. Take tomorrow off as a reward. Yes, I know it's Saturday tomorrow. What's the point? You had better explain yourself.

Isn't life Grand! Explanations are everywhere, from Astronomy to Zoology and all points in between, especially in Cybersecurity. We live, work, play, and die in a world nourished by explanations. We are born knowing all the answers and die asking all the questions. Why is that? We live in a faith filled world because so many explanations leave us wanting for better answers.

Cybersecurity is no exception. It brings the worst out of some people and also the best. We have the cybersecurity criminals and the cybersecurity protectors. Both have won some and both have lost some. The final result will depend greatly on the clarity and the insight of the explanations that emerge. Whatever these explanations become and to whomever they are delivered, they have to make sense so that everyone understands them first time around. If not, the Cybercriminals will have the advantage. Our explanations must be good enough to stop these criminals in their tracks before any damage is done and even before any security is violated. So, I think that we now have arrived at some final thought about the Potential, Possibilities, and Potency of Cybersecurity. Just remember as we continue, explanations have to be understood to be useful.

8: Some Final Thoughts About Insider Threats

Some people refer to Cybersecurity Criminals as Adversaries. This is too kind. They are not merely Adversaries. They are much more devious than this. They are not hobbyists. They are dangerous criminals who do not wish you well.

Insider Threats threaten your employer, your organization, your team, and you. It is a dirty and nasty business. It involves the following crimes:

- Abuse, Arson, Assault, Betrayal, Cheating, Computer Crime, Conspiracy, Corporate Crime, Corruption, Counterfeiting, Credit Card Fraud, Crimes Against Humanity, Cybercrime, Danger, Deception, Desecration, Disappointment, Discouragement, Discretion, Dishonesty, Deviousness, Eavesdropping, Embezzlement, Environmental Scheme Crimes, Extortion, False Accounting, Financial Crimes, Hate Crimes, Identity Cleansing, Impersonating a Public Official, Obsessive relational intrusion, Obtaining a money transfer by deception, Obtaining property by deception, Obtaining services by deception, Occupational crimes, Offences against public justice, Stalking, Tampering, Terrorism, Theft of Company Property, Theft of Government Property, Transnational Crime, Treachery, Wireless Identity Theft, and even Work at Home Schemes.

No wonder there are so many Cybercriminals today. They have so many crimes to choose from. WOW, think if the possibilities. The amazing thing is that this listing is incomplete. I did not list all of the dark possibilities such as espionage and foreign government intrusions. As you can see, there are a bunch of potential cybercrimes that encourage cybercriminals to act out their schemes. Computer Systems and networks are leveraged to assist criminals in executing their nefarious schemes. So much for progress. Have you ever considered all the possibilities out there for the criminal to carry out their agendas and how to defend yourself against them? Personally, I get about 125-150 spam calls a day. Much of it, including the scripts, the offers, the products, and whatever, are automated, very intrusive, and may even be illegal. They are a pain in the neck. While these calls may not be necessarily cybercriminals, they employ computer technology to be invasive to the extreme. I have little doubt that some of them are most involved in more nefarious possibilities. It is quite the global network engaging in such activities. Even though you will not know any of these people, they immediately start asking lots of personal questions as if it was their right. It is quite incredible actually.

Who are these people? What are really trying to do? Where did they get your phone numbers? Who provided the information to them? How do they know you rage? They may not be criminals but they certainly can be irritating, and they can be quite invasive. Today, this business model has certainly has become the global melting pot because a number of the callers are contacting us from other countries. It is, indeed, an international business.

It is uncomfortable to know that so many strangers have so many private and personal phone numbers. Doubtlessly, some of these people branch out to do "bigger and more lucrative business deals". Why not? Many other people do the same. Some of them even work for secret governmental agencies who are actively recruiting "Insiders" to assist them with their schemes.

With so much going in the Cyber Cosmos, Insiders Threats are expected. It is a percentage and possibility kind of thing that makes Insider Threats difficult to predict and even more difficult to predict. Predicting the who, when, and where of Insider Threats is not for children. It is a serious management obligation to be consistently aware of changes in their people. There are always signals of one kind or another telegraphed by their employees that alert manages can perceive. If they, themselves, are not the problems. If this is the case, thing can become really nasty very quickly as the stakes for loss dramatically increase day-by-day. The big question here for everybody, of course, is this: If there is so much possibility for the emergence of Insider Threats in the workplace, why are Insider Threats not so obvious to many of the people in the workplace? Indeed, why are they so difficult to detect? Obviously, some people are indeed very much aware of them but most seem to have little idea?

This is a good question that deserves a good and honest answer. Let's discuss it a bit, but first lets' take some time to briefly describe the different categories of Cybersecurity Insider Threats. There are only a few of them. Thank Goodness. I have seen classifications that ran from about six categories of Insider Threats to approximately ten categories of Insider Threats. How many of them can you identify? Incidentally, the most common number is two, that's right, only two categories of Insider Threats. However, do not panic. I am sure we can come up with several more by thinking like a Systems Scientist. Doesn't this make you feel better?

It includes corruption, espionage, degradation of resources, sabotage, terrorism, and unauthorized information disclosure. It can also be a starting point for cyber criminals to launch malware or ransomware attacks. As a number of organizations have learned, Insider threats are increasingly costly for organizations. A current list of Cybersecurity attack strategies includes the list below. Thee 21 Cybersecurity threats are merely an introduction to the possibilities.

After all, I identified about 46 crimes that are associated with Cybersecurity Threats, including the threats generated by "Insiders," trusted or otherwise. Actually, this list is still incomplete. Simply amazing how bad stuff propagates.

1. Denial-of-Service (DoS) attack DoS: This Cybersecurity attack overwhelms a system's resources to prevent the system from replying to legitimate service requests.
2. Distributed Denial-of-Service (DDoS): A DDoS attack is initiated using large collection of malware-infected host machines controlled by the attacker. In DDoS attacks, victim sites are unable to deliver service to those who request such services.
3. Man-in-the-Middle (MITM): In this case, attackers position themselves in the middle of two communicating parties to spy on them.
4. Phishing attacks: This cybersecurity attack occurs when a malicious actor sends emails that appear to be from legitimate sources to steal sensitive information.
5. Whale-phishing attacks: This is an attack that targets the senior leaders of an organization. This usually includes the Chief Executive Officer and the other "C" levels; but it can also refer to the most influential "mover and shakers" of the organization. These attacks generally demand a notable ransom.
6. Spear-phishing attacks: These are attacks against a specific target which is usually an individual. These attacks are often extremely elaborate.
7. Ransomware: This is the dream of the malware perpetrators. "I want your money, and I am going to get it, or no more system for you."
8. Password attacks: Here, criminals use several means to steal a password. They may even recruit someone in the workplace

to assist them using nefarious means.

9. SQL injection attacks: These are sensitive and time-consuming attacks. When they succeed, they are very costly. Data can disappear or be modified. The system is penetrated and the end-user may not know it; but the data and information is compromised as well as the control of the systems and its files. This is a fine time to be a "less privileged person"
10. URL interpretation/poisoning: Here, attackers use an URL address to gain access to sensitive data and information and do what they want. For highly sensitive info the Multi Factor Authentication (MFA is very helpful.
11. DNS spoofing: Here, using this method, a hacker alters Domain Name System (DNS) records to send traffic to a fake or "spoofed" websites.
12. Session hijacking: This is a complex approach that can be very successful because the server will use the hacker's IP address to verify its identity. Timing is everything.
13. Brute force attacks: Here the attacker guesses the login credentials of someone with access to the target system. Once they get it right, they are in. This is a common approach to Insider Threat success because the attacker is generally well-know and perceived as trustworthy. How about that?

1. Web attacks: Web attacks are cyber-attacks that target vulnerabilities found to exist by attackers in web-based applications. Hackers commonly employ Cross-Site Request Forgery (CSRF) attacks and parameter tampering to execute their web attacks.
2. Insider Threats: The name, Insider Threat, tells us where the attacker operates, namely, within the company where he or she works. Believe it or not, I am sorry to say that a company's own employee base presents a very serious cybersecurity risk to the safety and welfare of the company. Employees have the special access and perhaps privileges that criminals need. Think about the implications of a very knowledgeable Insider with an ax to grind. What a Threat!
3. Trojan Horses: In this case, a malicious program has been hidden inside another common or legitimate program. Under the right conditions, the hidden program, as the malware, often is used to enter a "backdoor" to gain entry into the system and engage in a hacking mission which could include theft. We can employ a Next Generation Firewall (NGFW) to examine data packets for potential Trojan Horse threats. Helen has nothing like back then. She would have loved these.
4. Drive-by attacks: Here, a hacker embeds intrusive/malicious code into an insecure website. Whenever an end-user visits that now infected site, the script is automatically executed on the visitor's computer, now infecting it as well. This situation is really a mean cyberattack. Simply by vising a site, the visitor's site becomes infected.
5. XSS attacks: With these Cross-Site Scripting attacks, the attacker sends malicious scripts using clickable content that gets sent to the target's browser. Ouch! These are particularly malicious and nefarious strategies used by hackers to

introduce a certain kind of Cyber Terror. These attacks can be very demoralizing. There is hope because there are ways to neutralize these attacks.

6. Eavesdropping Attacks: In these attacks, bad actors intercept traffic as it travels through the network. Here, attackers collect lots of fine information including: usernames, passwords, and other confidential information like credit cards.
7. Birthday Attack: Here, an attacker abuses hash algorithms, which, as a digital signature, verifies the authenticity of messages.
8. Malware Attack: Malware refers to "Malicious Software". Think about it. Malware is really on the rise and has significant impact on everything to do with computer technology and computer performance and computer communications, and.... Do you get the point? There are many, many, many bad actors out there who are just having some fun destroying and seizing what they can. Today, such people are busy getting their kicks reeking terribly expensive havoc on the world. Don't aid them.

What You Can Do

- Use firewalls that can detect malware
- Learn the software to avoid
- Learn what links not to click on
- Learn what links to verify
- Learn the emails to avoid
- Learn the attachments to avoid

Cybersecurity is Not a Walk in the Park

Insider Threats are Pervasive. Moral weakness is become more prevalent as companies expand the use of highly technical and complicated software that enables computer systems and networks to enable a data intensive world. I started my career in computers in 1962. We have always established security protocols for computers, systems, networks, and whatever. We have only partially succeeded with all of this Jazz.

People have always been the problem. Computers and software are easy when compared to the people problem we always face. It has been quite interesting when I think about my career and the people I have worked with and the places I have visited and the projects I have delivered. WOW! Where has the time gone? Here is the bigger question: Why are people still the problem? Cyber Security is a people problem. Insider Threat Prevention is a people problem. Insider Threat Mitigation is a people problem. Designing and integrating modern Information Technologies and Networks are different kinds of problems. These are solvable. These can be mastered. These can be eliminated. Technologies are easy. People Problems take a different approach. Of course they do. Some human beings develop values, morals, and ethics. Some human beings can become wise. But not all. Some human beings become Hackers, Insider Threats, Cyber Criminals, and careless human beings. Human beings respond to different imperatives. Some human beings become criminally pathological. Some can be helped. Many cannot. Many will not change. Some outgrow their lack of ethics. Many do not.

Cyber Security and the Potential of Artificial Intelligence

Today we live, work, and live our lives in a Technology-Centric world. Artificial Intelligence is not yet a serious technology, but it is getting there. Seriously! I hear it all the time: "Ray, A/I is the thing. A/I is the future. A/I is the game." Really? How much will it assist us with Insider Threat Prevention and Mitigation? This again is up to the designers of Artificial Intelligence, and us the technology consumers.

Ever here, there is a bunch of real moral and ethical challenges. If you truly want to know about Artificial Intelligence, learn all you can about the designer of a specific Artificial Intelligence System. Where they are in morals and ethics is where their A/I system will be.

Think about this if only for a moment: All intelligence is real intelligence. If it is intelligent, it is intelligent. If a kangaroo was Intelligent like a human being, it would be intelligent like a human being. But none of them are. You see, if a computer is intelligent life a human being, it would be intelligent like a human being. But some are in the labs now very, very intelligent. This means that the "computers" are indeed very, very intelligent like human beings in some capacities. You should realize that there is not such a thing as Artificial Intelligence. Real intelligence is real Intelligence. If the computer is intelligent like a human being, really like a human being, then this computer is indeed intelligent like a human being. So, watch out. Be careful. Tread lightly. Intelligence without morals and thus ethics is pathological. Are we building pathological systems? If so, they can, and probably will, turn against us. This is what intelligence without a moral code and ethical system does. Lying, cheating, manipulation are common among some people. These behaviors would be more so for A/I systems lacking an acceptable moral code.

Think about it. As Thomas Paine put it: "These are the times that try men's souls." They may very well be that if we fail to tread carefully with Artificial Intelligence. Simply look at the situation that we are experiencing today with Cybersecurity. This situation may become exponentially worse when we apply an advanced version of Artificial Intelligence in crucial ITP and ITM environments. Remember that intelligence is authentic intelligence even when it comes from a very advanced class of computer systems. And we are just getting started with an Artificial Intelligence super technology that can reason much faster than any human being. How does that grab you? You have to question whether such a system cares anything about the struggle between right and wrong. Perhaps we can use such a system to more quickly detect Insider Threats. What do you think?

Yea or nay? For the record, current approaches to Insider Threat Detection systems incorporates Artificial Intelligence (AI) and formal analytics to establish a baseline of activity for all end-users.

The Primary Categories of Insider Threats

Previously, I listed 21 different approaches to make Cybersecurity attacks. Generally, these attacks occur because they are malicious attacks by malicious. They also occur because people are sometimes careless people. Some are more difficult than others to resolve and some are more expensive than others to resolve. Surprise, surprise, surprise. What's new? Although there are so many of them happening, they only occur for a small number of reasons. For example, Insider Threats occur because of Carelessness, Negligence, and Maliciousness. That's it, three categories, many attack approach, and havoc. Let's Slip the Dogs of War" to defeat the Insider Threats. Whether the Cybersecurity threats are internal or externa, they always, and I mean always, involve employee directly or indirectly. For example, employees create Cybersecurity risks because of lack of:

- Training;
- Awareness;
- Caution;
- Laziness, and
- Carelessness

What Managers Can Do to Enhance Cybersecurity Success

Smart managers think about today, tomorrow and every day after that. They have to see the big picture well into the future. Whatever they do here, it will never be good enough. Cybersecurity success is complicated, very expensive, risky, and fleeting. Every day is a new challenge.

- Hire smart.
- Better educate employees as a regular function.
- Implement strong access controls and policies.
- Encrypt sensitive data.
- Maintain secure offsite backups.
- Regularly update software and eliminate vulnerabilities.
- Regularly engage in comprehensive audits.
- Deploy tested firewalls and endpoint protection.
- Segment networks.
- Engage in real-time systems assessment through 24/7 monitoring.
- Produce incident response plan.
- Regularly update incident response plan.

Change + Destroy + Steal + Exploit + Harm

This is very serious stuff. What do managers plan to do about it? They certainly cannot let it continue. Manager, you must get your act together. Left unchecked, it will eventually ruin you and your organization. The sad thing about this situation is that many organizations remain unaware that they are being damaged by their own people this way. It is so sad all aways around. Managers are not even aware that malicious attackers are busy stealing, selling destroying and disrupting sensitive information.

On the other hand, Negligent Insiders make many mistakes that degrade systems performance and damage the organization. Theya re the masters of "Human Error".

Executive Plan for Ensuring to ITP&M Success

So, here we are coming to the conclusion of this book about Cyber Security, especially Insider Threat Prevention or ITP. If an organization could deliver a potent ITP program that actually closes the gates to all unapproved and non-certified Insiders, life would become simpler and less expensive for the managers of those people. Think about it: certifying employees to gain access to the work areas. WOW! This is novel. It is also becoming quite necessary and quite necessary quite rapidly. The time is now. The Cyber Criminals are already disrupting the world.

We cannot keep sailing along as if today is 1975 still. It ain't! The Cyber Criminals are making life complicated by multiplying crime. It is time to stop whistling in the graveyard a midnight. The Cyber criminals are doing their thing 24X7. It is time to eliminate the laziness, carelessness and the maliciousness. It really is. I recognize that this is difficult stuff. We have to go on the offense to win the defense. This not to deny that we have made some progress in the battle to save our systems, but we are not there yet. We have to pile on and rub their faces in the mud. Naturally this raises the question: Ray, do you have a plan? That's your job, nit mine. There are several wonderful agencies out there that can assist you and even a few solid consultancies. For example, consider this definition courtesy of: https://www.cisa.gov/

> **Insider threats present a complex and dynamic risk affecting the public and private domains of all critical infrastructure sectors. Defining these threats is a critical step in understanding and establishing an insider threat mitigation program. The Cybersecurity and Infrastructure Security Agency (CISA) defines an insider threat as the threat that an insider will use their authorized access, intentionally or unintentionally, to do harm to the department's mission, resources, personnel, facilities, information, equipment, networks, or systems. Insider threats manifest in various ways: violence, espionage, sabotage, theft, and cyber acts.**

You see, even the government provides some guidance. Evey little bit helps. When it comes to Cyber Threats, there is plenty to know and plenty to do. Understanding at least this much, for your reference, I have put together a list of the tasks that an appropriate Plan of Action

(PoA) ought to include. Please be aware, this is not a detailed Plan of Action. It is merely a simple list of the topics that Insider Threat Prevention managers and planners should be discussing. I have used a traditional outline style for this PoA. So here goes:

Part One

- Identify the Technical Indicators of Insider Threats
- Design a Process for Preventing an Insider Threat?
    - Protecting Against Negligent Insider Threats
    - Preventing Malicious Insider Threats
- Learn How Identity Security Can Help Prevent Insider Threats
- Identify the Key steps to improving identity security include:
- Establish a Multi-Disciplinary Governance Group
- Establish Guiding Principles
- Focus on Protect vs. Punish?
- Develop ITP Cyber Security Policy
- Do Not Re-Invent the Wheel
- Avoid Zero-Tolerance Policies they are never impossible to resolve
- Liaise with Law Enforcement
- Address Legal Obligations
- Organize and Equip
- Integrate Information, Analysis
- Develop an Incident Response Plan
- Address Domestic Violence, It happens
- Mental Illness in Insider Threats
- Establish Reporting Pathways
- Employ Technology and Tools to Identify
- Concerning Behaviors
- Establish a Threat Assessment Methodology and Risk Rubric
- Establish a Multi-Disciplinary Threat Management Team possibly consisting of Chief Security Officer
- CIO & CISO?
- Operations & Admin Staff
- General Counsel

- Human Resources
- Legal Investigator
- Law Enforcement Officer
- Certified External Risk Screening Person
- Medial/Mental Health Counselor
- Several Insider Theat Analysts
- Supervisor & Co-Workers
- Trusted People (VV&T)
- Behavioral Scientist on a Threat Management Team
- Training for Threat Management Teams
- Documentation and Recordkeeping
- Training and Execution Plan/Budget
- Encourage a Culture of Reporting and Repairing
- Implement a Formal Training & Awareness Program to Match Your Requirements
- Evaluate and Improve Your ITP Program
- Conduct Reasonable Exercises
- Maintain the Program as Appropriate
- Provide 24/7 Oversight and Compliance

Part Two

Guideline for Establishing an Insider Threat Mitigation Program

- Develop ITM Presentation for C-Levels.
- Estimation of Potential Loss in Revenue, Market Share, and Competitive Edge, if any.
- Define the ITM Program for funding, Staffing, Training, and Monitoring, etc.
- Build Threat Management Team
- Define Audit Policies and Guidance
- Develop the ITM Program
- Determining which intellectual property was most valuable,
- Identify when the property was at risk,
- Develop a Risk Repository
- Track all projects and successful outcomes.
- Develop Communications Systems and Guidelines.
- Monitor all Impacts of the Program

Key Points

- Principles and Keys for Success
- Build the right culture for your organization
- Protect all valuables
- Be consistently adaptive
- Prevent, Prevent, Prevent
- Never overreact be solution oriented with expanded view

To Plan

- Recruit Recognized Leaders to Sponsor the program.
- Appoint a Point Executive for the ITP & ITM programs
- Initiate a Well-Informed Program Governance Team
- Publish the Guiding Principles of the Program
- Gain the Approval of Program from Senior Leaders
- Start Small and Go Big While Deepening Capabilities
- Identify, Track, and Monitor Use of Organization's Assets

Organize and Equip

- Employ the Fundamental Elements of the Program
- Employ Automated Tools & Techniques
- Use Skilled Investigators as Necessary
- Develop an Insider Threat Incident Response Plan
- Develop risk rubrics as evaluation tools
- Customize risk rubrics as necessary
- Design and Build a Threat Management Team
- Establish the Representation of Necessary Functional Disciplines

Train and Execute

- Form a Positive Reporting Culture
- Prevent Insider Threat Actions before They Impact Organization
- Continually Generate Insider Threat Awareness

Evaluate and Improve, Always Improve

- Regularly Complete and Fully Exercise the Insider Threat Mitigation Program.
- Designate Officials to Continually Conduct Independent Assessments.
- Update and Improve as Required.

Detecting and Identifying Insider Threats

- Resolve Grievance and Ideation
- Prepare Your Organization Adequately for Threat Detection
- Exploration the Targeted Environment
- Design Experiments to Uncover & Unmask Insider Threats
- Execute Strategies to Neutralize Insider Threats
- Eliminate Avenues of Insider Threat Escape
- Establish System of Threat Detectors
- Train People as Insider Threat Sensors
- Learn the Skills of Insider Threat Observation

Master the Skill of Observing Human Behavior

- Listen Carefully with Your Ears and Eyes to Perceived the Hidden Details.
- Monitor Insider Activity

Generating Risk Portfolios that Allow

- Control of Facility Access
- Identifying outlying behavior
- Perception of Threat Indicators
- Perception of Personal Indicators
- Clarify Background Indicators
- Perception of Behavioral Indicators
- Perception of Technical Indicators
- Perception of Organizational/Environmental Indicators

- Perception of Violence Indicators
- Perception of Domestic Abuse Indicator

- Perception of Terrorism Indicators
- Perception of Bias Incidents
- Perception of Hate Crime Indicators

Occasionally, good people get the shaft because someone was wrong about them. They have done nothing wrong but are accused of everything. Sometimes the Insider Threats are never recognized and get away completely free even though they did considerable damage. People simply did not like the "good people" personally. Is this right? Of course not. A solid ITP Program will prevent such mistakes from happening. One can hope. This is a good time to survey the environment and processes involved in organizing a potent ITP program. Let's begin by considering some of the key points below.

The use of a behavioral scientist in the assessment of potential Insider Threat Actors is a best practice for insider threat teams, especially for larger organizations.

Some Key Points

Cybersecurity People who know what they are doing understand that Insider Threats continually evolve in ways that can eventually reveal the Insider's unmasked Threat Behaviors that expose both the nature and goal of the Insider Threat Actor. It is not their motivators that unmask their grievances, it is the following indicators derived from life and work that may reveal the emerging Insider Threat Actor:

- Behaviors
- Context https://www.setci.org/
- Violence
- Predispositions,
- Technical Indicators,
- Stressors
- Capability

Assessing the Insider Threat

Insider Threat Assessment is challenging for several reasons. The focus of Insider Threat Prevention is not so much about Cyber this and that and security this and that. It is about the Insider Threat "Actor". It actually about gathering and analyzing freshly collected information about the "Actor". Think about it. Is he or she an immediate threat or no threat at all. Is this an unstable person or a misunderstood person? Is this person really an Insider Threat Actor?

Has the person been involved in any previous events or accidents that make him or her a target suspect? Or, are we climbing up the wrong tree? Does any relevant data and/or information from any relevant source point to this person as a possible Insider Threat Actor? What does the Insider Threat Report reveal? Is this a wrong turn? Do we have any information about a potential victim or Cyber Target? The thinking here is that the ITP Report will answer all of these question with a low margin of error. After all, it is this document that gains the commitment of the managers and Senior Executives.

Concluding Thoughts

We have come to the conclusion of this volume about Insider Threat Prevention or ITP. It has been an interesting journey. The kernel in the corn is what is really going on here. If ITP and ITM are simply about Insider Threats and their elimination, there are indeed innovative ways to do this for large corporations that management has not yet adopted. Currently when you look under the surface, what you discover is that people who are the Insider Threat present a mixed back of causal factors including greed, business opportunity, problems at home, workplace disagreements, unintended consequences, personal gain, stupidity, and on and on and on. It is about people making bad decisions, doing a bad job, people becoming their own worst enemies. and getting in their own ways.

In all of this, the situation that tells me how difficult Cybersecurity can be is the continuous range of ongoing Cybersecurity courses and seminars and presentations being delivered offering for everybody. The are presented as the "best new ways" to combat the strategies and threats of the many Cyber-Criminals out there. You see, they, too, can enroll in these courses just like they were anyone else. They, the Cyber Criminals, also can learn all about the new approaches and techniques devised to defeat the Cyber Criminals as they engage in their nefarious deeds. They too can learn all about the methods and techniques being developed to defeat themselves. Learning this, they, too, then can learn how to defeat these methods in the privacy and safety of their own homes, and stay at least one step ahead. So much for confidentiality. And so, it goes...

Common Cybersecurity Acronyms

ADA Americans with Disability Act

ASIS American Society for Industrial Security

BOLO Be-on-the-Lookout

CDSE Center for Development of Security Excellence

CIO Chief Information Officer

CISA Cybersecurity and Infrastructure Security Agency

CISO Chief Information Security Officer

CPG Comprehensive Preparedness Guide

CSO Chief Security Officer

DHS Department of Homeland Security

DLP Data Loss Prevention

DNS Domain Name System

DOD Department of Defense

EAP Employee Assistance Programs

FBI Federal Bureau of Investigation

FEMA Federal Emergency Management Agency

FOID Firearm Owners Identification

HR Human Resources

INSA Intelligence and National Security Alliance

IT Information Technology

IRM Incident Response Management

LEO Law Enforcement Officer

NaBITA National Behavioral Intervention Team Association

NCAVC National Center for the Analysis of Violent Crime

NIST National Institute of Standards and Technology

NITTF National Insider Threat Task Force

OSHA Occupational Safety and Health Administration

PAM Privileged Access Management

ROI Return on Investment

SEI Software Engineering Institute

SIEM Security Incident and Event Management
TOR The Onion Router (software name)
TSA Transportation Security Administration
UAM User Activity Monitoring
UBA User Behavior Analytics
USB Universal Serial Bus
USSS United States Secret Service
VPN Virtual Private Network

Conclusion to Part Three

Part One explored the Psychology of Insider Threat Prevention Cyber Terror by examining the impact of sociopathology on workplace relationships and the risk of malicious insiders. While introducing the Hallmarks of Continuous Performance Management (CPM), the author questioned Continuous Performance Management's resiliency in the face of the threat of Cyber Terror. It argued that Continuous Performance Management and Cyber Terror are both psychological phenomena coming from opposite ends of the behavioral spectrum.

Part Two in the series continued the theme of Continuous Performance Management-Insider Threat Prevention Cyber Security Unification by introducing the Newkirk Human Relationship Process Model as it begins to form the ITP Cyber Security strategies.

Part Three will introduce the strategies and methods that enable organizations to secure their CPM environments through ITPCS Unification without disrupting business operations. Here in this Series takes the challenge Insider Threat Prevention Cyber Terror head-on by introducing the vision of a Unified Continuous Performance Management and Insider Threat Prevention Cyber Security architecture derived from Behavioral Science.

Collectively, The Psychology of Insider Threat Prevention Cyber Security Sries examines the behavioral, social, technical, philosophical, managerial, strategic and operational considerations of such a large-scale program. It addresses the challenge of building new workplace relationships in organizations designed to combat Cyber Terror by building Insider Threat Prevention Cyber Security effectiveness in any organization.

Future Volumes in will examine the core components of any Insider Threat Prevention Cyber Security Program including Leadership, Communication, Training & Development, Governance, Risk Management, and Control.

Description of Terms

40 Inventive Principles: Refers to Altshuller's Collection of Principles derived from observation. People can employ the 40 Inventive Principles independently or with the Contradiction Matrix to solve problems creatively.

Abstract Term: Refers to a word or phrase that describes a generic feature, property or function that can identify an instant of one or more specific terms by adding or describing a relevant context. The same term can be specific in one case or abstract in another when used differently. For example, we can use the term "separate" abstractly one way while the term divide can be considered as specific another way.

Additional Function: Refers to a function that is not directly involved in delivering the main process but is merely associated with the main function or assists with achieving the main function.

Additional Inventive Principle: Refers to an Inventive Principle that people identified after Altshuller's defines his collection of 40 First Principles. Today, researchers have identified 10 additional Inventive Principles.

Administrative Contradiction: Refers to the description of an undesired effect or the definition of an essential inventive action that improves a situation in which a problem-solving method or a solution is unavailable.

Algorithm of Inventive Problem Solving (ARIZ): Refers to the most central analytical tool of Inventive Problem Solving, or TRIZ. As an algorithm, it consists of a specific sequence of logical processes, or steps, designed to analyze a vague or ill-defined problem and transform it as a distinct system conflict. Furthermore, analysis of the system conflict results in the formulation of the contradiction that ITP Cyber Security teams, using the separation principles and the enterprise's resources, must eliminate. This transformation is guided by the most fundamental concepts and methods of TRIZ including Ideal System, System Conflict, System Contradiction, the Su-Field analysis, the Inventive Standards and the Laws of Systems Evolution. Transformation occurs as the result of psychological and systemic operators.

Analogous Solution: Refers to a practice-based or inventive solution that emerges as teams resolve identical contradictions using the identical problem solving process used in previous solutions. Analogous Problems might also be defined by employing the same SuField model or the same function.

Anticipatory Failure Determination (AFD): Refers to a method and technique that identifies potential problems, including failures, either within an enterprise, i.e. Human Activity System, or its super-system caused by the technical system. AFD includes Failure Analysis and Prediction Analysis.

Anticipatory Failure Determination Failure Analysis: Refers processes that reveal causes of negative or undesired effects.

Anticipatory Failure Determination Prediction Analysis: Refers to process that predict potential negative or undesired effects.

Anti-Function: Refers to a function that is always opposite to a given function such to become more agitated vs. to become less agitated.

Anti-Principle: Refers to an Inventive Principle that consists of a problem-solving recommendation that is the opposite of a recommendation that delivers a known Inventive Principle. An anti-principle occurs such that the "Principle of Taking Away" becomes an anti-principle in relation to the "Principle of Adding to or Merging".

Anti-Process: Refers to a process that produces results that are opposite to another target process such as "agreeing" vs. "disagreeing", or "repairing" vs. "breaking". The anti-process" assists with formulating contradictions

Anti-System: Refers to a system that exists to oppose a function of another system. An anti-system may compete with the opposed system such that the closedness of an Insider Threat Prevention Cyber Security architecture may compete against the openness of a Continuous Performance Management.

Attribute: Refers to a fundamental quality of an architectural object that describes its interaction with other CPM and ITP CS objects. We associate attributes with types a range of values including Color, Weight, Complexity, and Phase state. The range of values may be linear, non-linear, or discrete. An attribute contains a parameter as subset of an attribute.

Auxiliary Function: Refers to a useful function of a component which behaves as a subsystem or a component of a system at a higher-level.

Base Technical System: Refers to a system that receives features from an alternative system. The base system is one of several systems selected for improvement.

Basic Function: Refers to a useful function targeted on an object of a system being analyzed.

Bell-Curve of Evolution: Refers to the cycles of growth or expansion and convolution or reduction.

Biological Effect (BE): Refers to an effect produced by a person or team that assists with the development of Inventive Problem Solving. The BE is at play whenever a team member leverages existing processes or actions present in the environment to improve Insider Threat Prevention Cyber Security. The team can collect these action steps to develop and execute Problem-Based Solutions.

Bi-System: Refers to systems that contain two or more identical, biased, or inverse components with functions or values of the same attributes that can be leveraged to create positive synergistic effects in which the results are more than the sum of their parts such that a considerable multiplication or decrease of a value of an attribute, or delivering a new property, or production of a new function.

Cardinal Virtues: Virtues are positive behaviors that become habits. The Cardinal Virtues include Justice, Fidelity, Self-Care, and Prudence. They are referred to as "Cardinal" because they are the hinges that lead to all the virtues.

Catalogue of Architecture Unification Effects: Refers to the CPM-ITPCS database of the Unification Program. The effects emerge from any involved discipline used in the Program. Designers organize the effects according to their generic functions. In each Program Catalogue, the effects are organized along different project groups. The following Catalogues of Program Effects are known: 1) Catalogue of Management Effects, 2) Catalogue of Network Effects, 3) Catalogue of Software Effects, 4) Catalogue of Social Effects, 5) Catalogue of Process Effects, 6) Catalogue of Cyber Security Effects, 7) Catalogues of Financial Effects, 8) Catalogues of Culture Effects, 9) Catalogue of Business Effects, 10) Catalogues of Training & Development Effects.

Cause Disadvantage: Refers to a disadvantage in the Unification Cause-Effect Chain that is a direct cause of a real versus apparent disadvantage.

Cause-Effect Chain: A visual model of a component of a Unification System being analyzed. The visual model maps the causes that directly or indirectly generate its disadvantage(s).

Cause-Effect Chains Analysis (CECA): Refers to an analytical process that identifies the principal disadvantages of the analyzed Unification system. We do this by building the cause-effect chains of disadvantages that link the disadvantages of concern to their fundamental

causes.

Computer Performance Evaluation (CPE): CPE is rigorous engineering experiment design to test the performance, reliability and capacity of an integrated computer system according to redefined external and internal acceptance criteria.

Design Inquiry: Iterative exploration of the systems, environments, spaces, dynamics, and models of design as the appropriate design inquiry architecture to produce a solution as a future system.

Existential Hunger: The innate and natural desire for union with other human beings. This refers to the human desire and capacity to form mutual relationships with human beings in a one-to-one and one-to-many correspondence, such as Social Connectivity, peer acceptance, affirmation.

Functional Relationship: Relationships in which human beings work together to achieve a mutual purpose or goal, as when sharing a social or professional project.

Human Activity System: A system in which the components are human beings engaging in processes of input, output, transformation, and feedback and adjustment.

Human Activity System Continua: The continuum of Human Activity Systems from open to closed, complex to simple (restricted), unitary to pluralist, and mechanistic to systemic.

Human Relationship Process Model: A relationships model that employs a Human Activity Systems view of transformation and growth.

Manipulative Relationship: A relationship emerging from Type One Existential Hunger in which other people are seen as means to an end regardless of the personal cost involved.

Metamethodology: METAM is a methodology for designing methodologies; HAS engage a MetaM to design a methodology appropriate to the type of HAS that is to be designed as an Information Systems. The MetaM is beyond any methodology. Close ties exist between methodologies and MetaM. Both Banathy and Checkland offer examples of MetaM. While Banathy (1989a) discussed a strategy for Design Inquiry as the design of design, Checkland (1981) offers a system for generating methodologies. Methodologies are valuable in that any advance in science is preceded by advances in methodology (Misiak & Sexton, 1966; Branden, 1974). However, "advances in methodology are preceded by advances in philosophy" (Newkirk, 1991, p. 34). For me, a MetaM is "a generalization of all methodologies as a second level abstraction to provide a MetaM of all methodologies" (Newkirk, 1991a, p. 28). Ontologically, as a second level abstraction, the metamethodology exists in the province of mathematics; retains intelligible matter; separates from common sensible matter; has the imagination as its end point; is a contingent system in that it cannot exist without individual sensible matter; and cannot be understood without intelligible matter (Hickey, 1976). MetaM rest on the bedrock of philosophical exploration and development. MetaM are required to design methodologies appropriate to a given problem situation. They are based on theory and practice, enhance system's evolution, organize methodologies, facilitate embedded systems building and support multiple paradigms (Newkirk, 1991a).

Methodology: A methodology can be hard or soft. Banathy (1988a) writes that a methodology "is defined as a set of coherent, related, and internally consistent methods applicable to pursuing disciplined inquiry" (p. 27). Checkland (1981) viewing methodology praxiologically, argues that "a methodology will lack the precision of a technique but will be a firmer guide to action than a philosophy" (p. 162). Flood and Carson (1988) discuss hard and soft systems methodologies by arguing that hard methodologies "set out to select an efficient means of achieving a known and defined end" (p. 107). Focusing on systems, Collen (1985) argues: "A systemic method is a formalized means of studying a system" (p. 536). He continues by arguing that "system methodology is the study of such methods, as well as the collective applications of such methods to the study of a human activity system" (p. 536). Dillon (1983) sees methodologies as imperfect. He argues that "Each is a product of the human mind and each is intended to bring some order out of the bewildering array of signals coming from the expanded sensory system. Each can form a mental image or model of the thing or event perceived, again it must be emphasized, from a particular perspective" (p. 11).

Methodology building is a design situation. It requires a design system to function as a methodology generating system, a HAS that engages a METAM to conduct Design Inquiry. To design a methodology, the designer must employ a METAM

Newkirk Model of Employee Engagement: Refers to the programs, processes, and activities that collectively work together to consistently build the performance of employees.

Newkirk Model of Workplace Relationships: The Relationship Model of Dr. Raymond L. Newkirk that establishes Existential Hunger as the driving force energizing the formation of all human relationships from Type One to Type Four.

Newkirk Relationships Process Model: Refers the levels of Existential Hunger and the nature and characteristics of the relationships they form as Human Activity Systems.

Objective Relationship: A relationship derived from Type One Existential Hunger that depersonalized members in the relationship by using them as objectives for attainment of goals.

Paradigm: Provides our perception of the world, how it works and what it contains in any given situation. We perceive the world within one world view or another which establishes any paradigm we may advocate for problem solving. Carrico (1989) describes a paradigm as a representation for the internal model that human beings employ to think about something. For Kuhn (1970), paradigms "define the legitimate problems and methods of a research field" (p. 10). Powers (1984), similar to Carrico above, argues that a paradigm "is a basic image which acts as an organizing and filtering agent, a socially accepted way of seeing, modelling, and communicating about reality" (p. 2). Powers sees a paradigm as a larger system consisting of three crucial subsystems: ontological, methodological, and epistemological. As a systemist, I see a paradigm as a suprasystem consisting of ontological, epistemological, and psychological subsystems which together inform a metamethodology for making sense out of the world. Our paradigms influence our efforts at designing our own futures through design inquiry. Carrico (1989) reasons that a paradigm serves as the representation for the internal model that we employ to think about something. Kuhn (1970) reasons that paradigms "define the legitimate problems and methods of a research field" (p. 10). Powers (1984) see a paradigm as a large philosophical system. As a systemist, I see a paradigm as a suprasystem consisting of ontological, epistemological and psychological subsystems which together inform a metamethodology as a design inquiry for making sense out of the world. Our paradigm influences our efforts of designing on own future through design inquiry. Others see paradigms as metaphorical (Morgan, 1986).

Principles, Laws, Corollaries and Guidelines: The Systems Approach is operationalized through its various dictates, assumptions, pre-suppositions, and guiding notions as expressed in the form of principles, laws, corollaries and guidelines (Yourdon, 1989a). This "legal" and "disciplined" foundation derived from GST stresses the nature of the systems approach as an expanded encounter with the world being perceived in the form of dynamical systems in interaction and interdependence through the interconnectedness of subsystems rather than as a background of static, discrete and non-interrelated components in isolation (Yourdon, 1989a). An important corollary of the system approach is that as systems thinkers, we come to appreciate the uniqueness of an entity as a member of any system. If it is correct that a system is changed whenever a component or subsystem enters the system or leaves it, the component must be unique (Mayon-White and Morris, 1982). From the human science perspective studying both the expanded domain of HAS and the discrete organization structures and functions of traditional Organization Development, this corollary defends the uniqueness and indispensability of every person. Every human person brings something unique into their systems. This something unique makes the system other than what it previously was (Mayon-White & Morris, 1982). The axioms, propositions, principles, laws, corollaries, and guidelines of the system approach are derived from the basic definition of the concept system. Bertalanffy (1950), Ashby (1956), Miller (1956), Checkland (1981), Myon-White and Morris (1983), Bogdanov (1984), Christakis (1985) and Warfield (1987) have all made their contributions. As the system movement evolves, the laws and principles developed within this perspective will gain increasing weight and influence. Although the dictates of the systems perspective lack empirical credibility, experience with them indicates that they contain logical content. Checkland (1981) reasoned that: "As the use of systems concepts in problem-solving is developed we may expect a parallel emergence of laws deriving from the logic of the use of systems ideas" (p. 234). These systems ideas are derived from the various systems perspectives that are evolving as a new paradigm of disciplined inquiry. Systems principles are implicit in many new theories of corporate rebirth.

Spiritual Personal Relationship: A high-order relationship derived from Type Four Existential Hunger that leads individuals to personal-spiritual transformation and the attainment of uniquely spiritual values.

- Level One Existential Hunger: Fundamental human drive that leads to the formation of self-centered relationships.

- Level Two Existential Hunger: Higher-level human drive to form relationships in which people may participate in attaining mutual goals.

- Level Three Existential Hunger: Higher-Level human drive to form relationships in which the categories of love emerge as human beings become ends in themselves rather than means to ends.

- Level Four Existential Hunger: Highest level of human relationship in which human beings seek out and pursue transformation of values and activities to experience deepest meanings of life, love, and relationships.

System: Mayon-White and Morris (1982) reasoned that a system is an assembly of components of particular interest to someone that are connected in an organized way for doing something. The components are affected by being in the system in such a way that the system is changed if any component leaves it. Systems are classified as natural system, designed systems, human activity systems, and social systems. Systems can be either hard or soft, designed physical systems or designed abstract systems. Some even authorities claim that systems exist which are beyond human knowledge; these are the transcendental systems (Checkland, 1981). In LST (Miller, 1988), systems consist of 19 subsystems.

Systems Design and Relevant Dynamics: Systems Design is a disciplined inquiry consisting of specialized techniques, general rules and universal principles. Banathy (1984) writes that "design is creative, disciplined, and decision-oriented inquiry carried out in iterative cycles. During these cycles, we develop design solutions by exploring three `spaces' that surround the design solution space: (a) the design knowledge space, (b) the design problem space, and (c) the design exploration space" (pp. 1-11). Design systems work within the spaces of design to produce a desired system. Collen (1990) reasons that "Systems design is an ongoing activity which requires the participation of all stakeholders if a HAS is to evolve" (p. 4). Collen refers to the systems design methodology as the "Systems Design Journey" (p. 4) to reflect the continuous or evolutionary nature of design as distinct from planning. The evolutionary nature of design flows from the dynamics occurring within the design experience. Two significant dynamics of design have been identified by Banathy (1984) as divergence and convergence. Design commences with an image of the future system and works to achieve it through iterations of divergence and convergence. The outcome of the design experience is a description of a new system to be implemented.

Systems Perspectives: The systems approach is engaged in a continuous debate. Debate rages over the very efficacy of the movement itself. Some fear that it may be just a new way of expressing old ideas. Others wonder if the systems approach is so general as to be vague, vacuous, and meaningless. Some argue over the best approach to systems. Just as the systems perspective is a way of perceiving the world, there exist several ways of perceiving systems. Churchman (1979) writes that "the systems approach really consists of a continuing debate between various attitudes of mind with respect to society" (p. xi). He reasons that many systems debaters exist who fall into one of four classes of systems thinkers: (1) efficiency thinkers who study trouble spots; (2) science advocates who build objective models; (3) humanists who consider values while encouraging noninterference; (4) antiplanners who encourage experience at the expense of other rational approaches.

Workplace Relationships: Refers to associations and relationships formed in the workplace to meet personal and professional goals derived from Type One to Type Four Existential Hunger.

References & Historical Bibliography

This section provides a historical Reference and Bibliography that takes you back to the beginning when visions like Networked Information Systems, Continuous Performance Management and Insider Threat Prevention Cyber Security first began to emerge and brings you up to today. It introduces many of the thinkers and their ideas and concepts that informed the emergence and subsequent evolution of Insider Threat Prevention Cyber Security (ITPCS). At its best, ITPCS is a difficult discipline that, fortunately for us, has amassed a wonderful volume of insight over the years.

Mastery of the Psychology of Insider Threat Prevention Cyber Security is not an overnight project. Although each company suffers its own ITPCS concerns, they all share common challenges that elicit shared strategies and responses. As we have seen in Part One, Continuous Performance Management shares several Hallmarks that make ITP Cyber Security more difficult to enforce such as trust and openness and minimal management. Other organization initiatives and architectures have issues that also complicate the enforcement of ITP Cyber Security.

Many, if not most, people today are unaware of the breadth and depth of the conceptual universe that forms a viable, potent, and successful Insider Threat Prevention Cyber Security Program. Actually, several dozen disciplines come together to form resilient ITP Cyber Security. These range from Software Development, Program and Project Management, Hardware Systems Engineering, Budgeting, Finance, Strategic Thinking, Operations Management, Network Management, Version Control, and Human Resource Management to Behavioral Science, Sociology, Theology, Forensic Psychology, Personality and Trait theories, Systems Thinking, Human Activity Systems Design, Philosophy, Physics, Mathematics, Management, Organization Design, Enterprise Architecture Planning, Critical

Theory, Ideology Critique, Training and Development, Communications, Methodology Design, Product Development and several others. I am sure you get the idea.

ITP Cyber Security is a complex challenge that people generally under-conceptualize. Getting it right demands significant change throughout the enterprise. The key word here is "PREVENTION". I am not talking about repair, correction, or making something less painful which is common with mitigation strategies. Mitigation is the effort to reduce loss of life and property by lessening the impact of disasters. II am speaking of Insider Threat Prevention Cyber Security. I mean stopping it in its tracks before it happens. This is hard to do, but it can be done.

Insider Threat Prevention is essential because such malicious insider attacks can destroy an entire enterprise in a very, very short time. While external intrusions are dangerous, very expense, and threatening, they rarely destroy an entire enterprise. Organizations recover from them. ITP Cyber Security is far difference because an increasing percentage of them render their targets useless, forever. Executive shave to think differently about Insider Threats, and implement enterprise architecture that actually prevent them while concurrently enhancing business operations. Success in the ear of Cyber Terror is indeed the brave new world.

As you understand more clearly the danger of insider attacks, you will also begin to recognize how complex this problem really is. Many disciplines come together to produce an Architecture that unifies enterprise models and Insider Threat Prevention Cyber Security models. An effective ITP Cyber Security solution presents a challenge of environmental unification that is well beyond the common practices of systems integration. This requires a knowledge base derived from the contribution of the thirty plus disciplines identified above.

Aamodt, Agnar: A Knowledge-Intensive, Integrated Approach to Problem Solving and Sustained Learning.

References

Achinstein, Peter (1983) The Nature of Explanation. New York: Oxford University Press.

Ackoff, R. L. (1979, July). The Future of Operational Research is Past. In R. E.

Ackoff, R.L. (1981). Creating the Corporate Future. New York: John Wiley & Sons.

Ackoff, R. L. (1982). On the Hard Headedness and Soft Headedness of M. C. Jackson. Journal of Applied Systems Analysis, 9.

Ackoff, R. L. (1991). Ackoff's Fables: Irreverent Reflections on Business and Bureaucracy. New York: John Wiley & Sons, Inc.

Ackoff, R. L., & Emery, Fred E. (1972). On Purposeful Systems. Seaside, CA: Intersystems Publications.

Adams, Kevin: Towards a System of Systems Methodologies, Once Again. Old Dominion University.

Adams, Kevin (2012): Systems Theory: A Formal Construct for Understanding Systems. Old Dominion University.

Adam, Nabil R. & Wortmann, John C. (1989, December). Security-Control Methods for Statistical Analysis Databases: A Comparative Study. ACM Computing Surveys, 21(4), pp. 515-556.

Altshuller G.S. (1998). The Innovation Algorithm: TRIZ, Systematic Innovation, and Technical Creativity. Worcester, MA: Technical Innovation Center.

Altshuller G.S. (1994). Creativity as an Exact Science. New York, NY: Gordon & Breach.

Altshuller G.S. (2003). To find the Idea. 1st edition: Novosibirsk, Nauka, 1993, 2nd edution: Petrozavodsk, Scandinavia, 2003 (in Russian: Альтшуллер Г.С. Найти Идею, Новосибирск: Наука, 1-е издание, 1986; 2-е издание, 1991; 3-е изд., доп., Петрозаводск: Скандинавия,).

Altshuller G.S. (1989). Search for New Ideas: From Insight Towards Technology: Theory and Practice of Inventive Problem Solving. Kishinev, Karta Moldavenjaske, (In Russian: Альтшуллер

Г.С., Злотин Б.Л., Зусман А.В. - Поиск новых идей: от озарения к технологии (теория и практика решения изобретательских задач). - Кишинев: Картя Молдовеняскэ.

Altshuller G.S. Vertkin I.M. (1994). How to Become a Genius: Life Strategy of Creative Personality. Minsk, Belarus, 1994 (In Russian: Альтшуллер Г.С., Верткин И.М. Как стать гением: Жизненная стратегия творческой личности. - Минск: Беларусь).

Altshuller G.S. (1982). Biological Effects as Analogy of Physical Effects, Baku, 1982 (In Russian: Альтшуллер Г.С. Биологические эффекты как аналогия физических эффектов, Баку.)

Altshuller, G.S. (2013). Altshullers's Foundation: Main Terms of TRIZ. Version 1.0 (In Russian: Фонд Альтшуллера: Основные термины ТРИЗ/версия 1.0.

Amabile, Teresa M. (1983). The Social Psychology of Creativity. New York: Springer-Verlay

Andrews, Gregory R. (1991, March). Paradigms for Process Interaction in Distributed Programs. ACM Computing Surveys, 23 (1), pp. 49-90.

Andriole, Stephen J. (1985). Applications in Artificial Intelligence. Princeton: Petrocelli Books.

Andriole, Stephen J. (1986a). Microcomputer Decision Support Systems: Design, Implementation and Evaluation. Wellesley, MA: QED Information Sciences.

Andriole, Stephen J. (Ed.) (1986b). Software Validation, Verification, Testing and Documentation. Princeton: Petrocelli Books.

Annual Threat Report (2018). Produced by eSentire Threat Intelligence.

Anton, Corey (2015). A Heuristic Sketch of Lee Thayer's Systems Theory Orientation to Human Communication: Reflections on the Range of Open Systems. Grand Valley State University,

Aquinas, Thomas, Saint (1952). The Summa Theologica. Daniel J. Sullivan (Tr.). Chicago: The University of Chicago (The Great Books Edition), William Benton Publisher,

Aquinas, Saint Thomas, De Veritate, Summa Theologiae, I, q. 14.

Aquinas, Thomas, St.: Summa Theologica, I, Q. 85. Art 7.

Argyris, C; Schön, Donald A. (1985) Strategy, Change and Defensive Routines. Ballinger: Cambridge, MA.

Argyris, Cris (1970). Intervention Theory and Method. Reading, MA: Addison-Wesley.

Argyris, Chris, et al., (1985). Action Science. San Francisco: Jossey-Bass.

Aristotle (1952). Works of Aristotle. W. D. Ross (Ed.), 12 Vols. Oxford: Clarendon, Press.

Armstrong, A. H. (1949). An Introduction to Ancient Philosophy. Chicago: Newman Press.

Arraj, James. Jungian Spirituality: The Question of Victor White, Spirituality Today, Autumn 1988, Vol. 40 No. 3, pp. 249-261.

Ashby, W.R. (1956). An Introduction to Cybernetics. London: Chapman and Hall.

Ashby, W.R. (1958). Requisite Variety and Its Implications for the Control of Complex Systems. Cybernetics, 1, pp. 1-17

Association For Computing Machinery. (1990, October). Proceedings of the Conference on Computer-Supported Cooperative Work, October 7-10, 1990 Los Angeles, CA. Sponsored by ACM SIGCHI & SIGOIS.

Augustine, of Hippo (1981). Basic Writings of St. Augustine. Oates & Whitney (Tr.). New York: Baker Books.

Auletta, Gennaro (2005). The Trialistic Structure in Physics, Spiritual Information: 100 Perspectives on Science and Religion, Charles L. Harper, Jr. ed. Philadelphia, PA: Templeton Foundation Press, 2005.

Austin, Charles F. (1966). Management's Self-Inflicted Wounds: A Formula for Managerial and Executive Self-Analysis. New York: Holt, Rinehart and Winston.

Ayer, Steve J. & Patrinostro, Frank S. (1992). Software Configuration Management Identification, Accounting, Control, & Management. New York: McGraw-Hill, Inc.

Baker, Richard H. (1985). The Computer Security Handbook. Blue Ridge Summit, PA: TAB Professional and Reference Books.

Banathy, Bela (1973). Developing a Systems View of Education. Seaside, CA: Intersystems Publications.

Banathy, Bela (1979). The Dynamics of Integrative Design. General Systems Research, a Science, a Methodology, a Technology. Louisville: Society for General Systems Research.

Banathy, Bela (1983). Systems Behavior. San Francisco: Saybrook Institute.

Banathy, Bela (1984). Systems Design in the Context of Human Activity Systems. San Francisco: International Systems Institute.

Banathy, Bela (1986a). The Design of Design Inquiry in the Context of Human Activity Systems. San Francisco: Far West laboratory for Educational Research and Development.

Banathy, Bela (1986b, October). A Systems View of Development. U.N. Educational, Scientific and Cultural Organization Symposium: Meeting of experts on goals of development. Budapest.

Banathy, Bela (1987a). The Design of Evolutionary Guidance Systems. San Francisco: Saybrook Institute

Banathy, Bela (1987b). The Characteristics and Acquisition of Evolutionary Competence. World Futures, 23, pp. 123-144.

Banathy, Bela (1987c). Choosing Design Methods. San Francisco: Far West Laboratory & Saybrook Graduate School.

Banathy, Bela (1988a). Matching Design Methods to System Type. San Francisco: Saybrook Institute.

Banathy, Bela (1988b). Goals of Development. Paris: U.N. Educational, Scientific and Cultural Organization.

Banathy, Bela (1989a). Design: A Journey to Create the Future, A Map Of The Journey. Carmel: Far West Laboratory and Saybrook Institute.

Banathy, Bela (1989b). The Design of Evolutionary Guidance Systems. Systems Research, 4.

Banathy, Bela (1990). Design: A Journey to Create the Future, A Map of The Journey. R. Trappi (Ed.), Cybernetics and Systems, 1990: Proceedings of the Tenth European Meeting on Cybernetics and Systems Research. Singapore: World Scientific, pp. 197-204.

Banathy, Bela (1991). Systems Design of Education: A Journey to Create the Future. Englewood Cliffs: Educational Technology Publications.

Banathy, B. H. & Mills, S. R. (1985). The Application of Living Systems Process Analysis in Education. ISI Monograph 85(7), pp. 1-16.

Barr, Avron & Feigenbaum, Edward A. (1981). The Handbook of Artificial Intelligence, Volume 1. Los Altos, CA: William Kaufmann, Inc.

Barr, Avron & Feigenbaum, Edward A. (1982). The Handbook of Artificial Intelligence, Volume 2. Los Altos, CA: William Kaufmann, Inc.

Bateson, Gregory (1973). Steps to an Ecology of Mind. London: Paladin.

Bateson, Gregory (1979). Mind and Nature: A Necessary Unity. New York: E. P. Sutton.

Bayraktar, B.A., H. Muller-Merbach, J. E. Fricchione, Gregory L. (2005). Of Monocytes and the Spiritual Man, Spiritual Information: 100 Perspectives on Science and Religion, Charles L. Harper, Jr. ed. Philadelphia, PA: Templeton Foundation Press, 2005, pp. 400-405.

Beckhard, Richard (1967). The Confrontation Meeting. Harvard Business Review, XLV(2), 149-153.

Beckhard, Richard (1969). Organization Development: Strategies and Models. Reading, MA: Addison-Wesley Publishing Company.

Beckhard, Richard & Harris, Reuben (1977). Organizational Transitions: Managing Complex Change. Reading, MA: Addison-Wesley Publishing Company.

Beckhard, Richard & Pritchard, Wendy (1992). Changing the Essence: The Art of Creating and Leading Fundamental Change in Organizations. San Francisco: Jossey Bass Publishers.

Bellefontaine, Elizabeth. A Spirituality of Meaningful Experiences: Some Biblical Lesson, Spirituality Today, Autumn 1988, Vol. 40 No. 3, PP. 196-207.

Belnap and Steele (1976) The Logic of Questions and Answers. New Haven: Yale University

Bennett, Roger (1989). Personal Effectiveness. London: Kogan Page Ltd.

Bennis, Warren (1969). Organization Development: Its Nature, Origins, and Prospects. Reading, MA: Addison-Wesley Publishing Company.

Bennis, Warren (1989a). Why Leaders Can't Lead: The Unconscious Conspiracy Continues. San Francisco: Jossey-Bass Publishers.

Bennis, Warren (1989b). On Becoming a Leader. Menlo Park: Addison-Wesley Publishing Company.

Bennis, Warren & Nanus, Burt (1985). Leaders The Strategies for Taking Charge. New York: Harper & Row, Publishers.

Bernstein, R. J. (1983) Beyond Objectivism and Relativism. Basil Blackwell: Oxford.

Bertalanffy, L. von (1950). The Theory of Open Systems in Physics and Biology. Emery (Ed.) (1969) Systems Thinking. Harmondsworth, England: Penguin.

Bertalanffy, L. von (1968). General Systems Theory. New York: Braziller.

Beruvides, Mario Ph.D. & Cantu, Jaime (2013). Isomorphological Analysis: The Theory of It All. Texas Tech University

Boehm, B. A. (1981). Software Engineering Economics. Englewood Cliffs: Prentice-Hall, Inc.

Bogdanov, A. (1984). Essays in Tektology: The General Science of Organization. Seaside, CA: Intersystems Publications.

Boghossian, Paul A. (2007). Fear of Knowledge:Against Relativism and Constructivism. Oxford, England: Oxford University Press.

Boulding, Kenneth E. (1985). Human Betterment. Beverley Hills: Sage Publications.

Bowers, Todd, David. An Ontology for a Critical Systems Paradigm. Thesis submitted for the M.Phil./Ph.D. Upgrade. Centre for Systems Studies, Hull U. Business School. California State Polytechnic U. at Pomona January, 2009

Bowers, Todd D. (2008) An Ontology for a Critical Systems Paradigm. Ph.D. Upgrade. Hull University Business School, Unpublished.

Bowers, Todd D. (2011) Ontological Support for Multiparadigm Multimethodologies: Isomorphic Process–Structures and the Critical Moment. Proceedings of the 54th Meeting of the International Society for the Systems Sciences. Hull, U.K.

Bowers, Todd D. Ph.D. (2012) Towards a Framework for Multiparadigm Multimethodologies. Centre for Systems Studies, Hull University Business School, University of Hull: Hull.

Bowers, Todd David, Ph.D: Developments in Critical Systems Theory: On Paradigms and Incommensurability. Universidad del Norte – Barranquilla

Bowker, John W. (2005). God, Spiritual Information, and Downward Causation, Spiritual Information 100 Perspectives on Science and Religion, Charles L. Harper, Jr. (Ed.). Philadelphia, PA: Templeton Foundation Press. (pp. 479-483).

Boyd, Robert, D. & Myers, J. Gordon. Overcoming Leadership Scarcity: Discerning the Spiritual Journey, Spirituality Today, Autumn 1987, Vol. 39, pp. 225-240.

Branden, Nathaniel (1973). The Psychology of Self-Esteem. New York: Bantam Books.

British Telecommunications plc: How We Stay Ahead of a Changing Threat Landscape. (2018) Registered office: 81 Newgate Street, London EC1A 7AJ.

Brody, Baruch A. (1970) Readings in the Philosophy of Science. Englewood Cliffs, N.J.: Prentice Hall

Bromberger, Sylvain (1966) "Why-Questions," In Baruch A. Brody, ed., Readings in the Philosophy of Science, 66-84. Englewood Cliffs: Prentice Hall, Inc.

Bucker, Bill (2003). Spiritual Development and the Epistemology of Systems Theory, Journal of Psychology and Theology Vol. 31, 2003

Burrell, Gibson &Morgan, Gareth (1979) Sociological Paradigms and Organizational Analysis. Heinemann: London. Management Science, 17, B37–B53.

Capra, Fritjof (1982). The Turning Point. New York: Simon & Schuster

Capra, Fritjof (1991). The Tao of Physics, third edition. Boston: Shambhala.

Capra, Fritjof and **Steindl-Rast** (with Thomas Matus) (1991). Belonging to the Universe. San Francisco: Harper.

Cavallo (Ed.), Systems Research Movement: Characteristics, Accomplishments and Current Developments. Binghampton, NY: Society for General Systems Research.

CERT National Insider Threat Center. Common Sense Guide to Mitigating Insider Threats, Sixth Edition. December **2018**

Checkland, Peter B. (1981). Systems Thinking, Systems Practice. Wiley: Chichester.

Christakis, A. N. (1981). High Technology Participative Design: The Space Based Laser. Proceedings of the Annual Meeting, Society for General Systems Research. Louisville, KY.

Churchman, C. West (1970). Operations Research as a Profession.

Churchman, C. W. (1971). The Design of Inquiring Systems. New York: John Wiley & Sons.

Churchman, C. W. (1979a). The Systems Approach and Its Enemies. New York: Basic Books. Churchman, C. W. (1979b). The Systems Approach. New York: Dell Publishing Company.

Churchman, C. W. (Ed.) (1989). The Well-Being of Organizations. Seaside, CA: Intersystems Publications.

Codd, E. F. (1990). The Relational Model for Database Management, Version 2. Menlo Park: Addison-Wesley Publishing Company.

Collen, Arne (1985). Experimental Method within Systems Methodology: The Case for and against. B. Banathy, (Ed.). Proceedings of the Society for General Systems Research, 1, pp. 536-539.

Collen, Arne (1987, October). Living Systems Process Analysis for Program Evaluation. A paper presented at the annual meeting of the American Evaluation Association in Boston.

Collen, Arne (1988, May). Living Systems Methodology for Organizational Design and Redesign. Paper presented at the meetings of the International Society for General Systems Research, St. Louis, Missouri.

Collen, Arne (1990, April 10). Evolutionary Guidance Systems and Systems Design. A paper presented at the Tenth European Meeting on Cybernetics and Systems Research in Vienna.

Collen, Arne (1992). Methodological Perspectives on Human Systems, Design, and Learning for a More Global Ethic. San Francisco: Saybrook Institute.

Collen, Arne, Ph.D. & Newkirk, Raymond L. (1992). Cybernetics, Living Systems Theory, and Organizational Behavior. San Francisco & Concord, California: Saybrook Institute & Systems Management Institute (Paper for 13th international Congress on Cybernetics).

Collins, Robin A. (2005). Design and the Designer, Spiritual Information: 100 Perspectves on Science and Religion, Charles L. Harper, Jr. ed. Philadelphia, PA: Templeton Foundation Press.

Conrad, James W. (1988). Handbook of Communications Systems Management. Boston: Auerbach Publishers, Inc.

Conrad, James W. (1989). Handbook of Communications Systems Management, 1989 Yearbook. Boston: Auerbach Publishers, Inc.

Conrad, James W. (1990a). Handbook of Communications Systems Management, 1990-1991 Yearbook. Boston: Auerbach Publishers, Inc.

Conrad, James W. (1990b). Handbook of Communications Systems Management: Communications Standards. Boston: Auerbach Publishers, Inc.

Constantine, Larry (1995). Constantine on Peopleware, Yourdon Press.

Constantine, Larry & Ambler, Scott W. (2002). The Unified Process Transition and Production Phases Best Practices in Implementing the UP. CMP Books, Kansas

Craig & Houston-Ludlam (1989, May 25). A Psychological Framework for Testing. Sixth International Conference on Testing Computer Software, Ann Harbor, MI: Tec-Ed Technical Publications and Graphics Services.

Csanyi, Vilmos (1982). General Theory of Evolution. Budapest: Akademiai Kiado.

Date, Christopher J. (1975). An Introduction to Database Systems. Addison-Wesley Publishing Company.

Date, Christopher J. (2001). The Database Relational Model: A Retrospective Review and Analysis: a Historical Account and Assessment of E.F. Codd's Contribution to the Field of Database Technology. Addison-Wesley.

Date, Christopher J. (2005). Database in Depth: Relational Theory for Practitioners. O'Reilly.

Date, Christopher J. (2006). The Relational Database Dictionary: A Comprehensive Glossary of Relational Terms and Concepts, with Illustrative Examples. O'Reilly.

Date, Christopher J. (2016). Type Inheritance and Relational Theory: Subtypes, Supertypes, and Substitutability. O'Reilly.

Date, Christopher J. (2009). SQL and Relational Theory: How to Write Accurate SQL Code. O'Reilly.

Davidow, William H. & Malone, Michael S. (1992). The Virtual Corporation: Structuring and Revitalizing the Corporation for the 21st Century. New York: Harper Collins Publishers.

Davino, Louis. Francis of Assisi: Metaphor of Franciscan Maturity, Spirituality Today, Autumn 1987, Vol. 39, pp. 241-249.

Defense Systems Management College (1988). Test and Evaluation Management Guide. Fort Belvoir, VA: Defense Systems Management College.

Defense Systems Management College (1989a). Defense Manufacturing Management: Guide for Program Managers Fort Belvoir, VA: Defense Systems Management College.

Defense Systems Management College (1989b). Systems Engineering Management Guide. Fort Belvoir, VA: Defense Systems Management College.

Defense Systems Management College (1990). Scheduling Guide for Program Managers. Fort Belvoir, VA: Defense Systems Management College.

Defense Systems Management College (1986b). Integrated Logistics Support Guide. Fort Belvoir, VA: Defense Systems Management College.

Defense Systems Management College (1987). Guide for the Management of Multinational Programs. Fort Belvoir, VA: Defense Systems Management College.

Defense Systems Management College (1987) Risk Management Concepts and Guidance. Fort Belvoir, VA: Defense Systems Management College.

DeMarco, Tom (1978). Structured Analysis and System Specification. Yourdon, New York.

DeMarco, Tom (1982). Controlling Software Projects, Yourdon Press.

DeMarco, Tom (1987). Peopleware: Productive Projects and Teams, Barnes & Noble.

DeMarco, Tom (2001). Slack:Getting Past Burnout, and the Myth of Total Efficiency. Boradway Books, New Your, New York.

DeMarco, Tom (2003). Waltzing with Bears: Managing Risks on Software Projects, Barnes & Noble

Denton, Michael, J. (2005). Henderson's Fine-Tuning Argument, Spiritual Information: 100 Perspectives on Science and Religion, Charles L. Harper, Jr. ed. Philadelphia, PA: Templeton Foundation Press, 2005.

Derek Melber, MVP (2020): Detecting Insider Threats and Attacks, Manage Engine Special Edition. John Wiley & Sons, New Jersey, 2020

Dickinson, Brian (1989). Developing Quality Systems: A Methodology Using Structured Techniques. New York: McGraw-Hill Book Company.

Dickinson, Brian (1980). Developing Structured Systems: A Methodology Using Structured Techniques. New York: Yourdon Press.

Dinsmore, Paul C. (1984). Human Factors in Project Management. New York: American Management Association Publications Group.

Domb, Ellen & Rantanen, Kalevi (2002): 40 Principles for Innovative Problem Solving. TRIZ, CRC Press.

Doohan, Leonard. Current Trends Scripture and Contemporary Spirituality, Spirituality Today, Spring 1990, Vol. 42 No. 1, pp. 62-74.

Downey, Michael. Current Trends Understanding Christian Spirituality: Dress Rehearsal for a Method, Spirituality Today, Fall 1991, Vol. 43 No. 3, pp. 271-280.

Drack, Manfred & Pouvreau, David (2006). On the History of Ludwig von Bertalanffy's "General Systemology", and on Its Relationship to Cybernetics Part I: Elements on the Origins and Genesis of Ludwig von Bertalanffy's "General Systemology." International Journal of General Systems, 44:5, 523-571,

Drack, Manfred & Pouvreau, David (2015). On the History of Ludwig Von Bertalanffy's "General Systemology", and on Its Relationship to Cybernetics – Part III: Convergences and Divergences. International Journal of General Systems, 44:5, 523-571

Drucker, Peter (1989). The New Realities. New York: Harper & Row Publishers.

Drucker, Peter (1992). Managing for the Future: The 1990s and Beyond. New York: Truman Talley Books/Dutton.

Duffey, Michael K. Called to be Holy:The Reconvergence of Christian Morality and Spirituality, Spirituality Today, Winter 1986, Vol. 38, pp. 349-360.

Duhem, Pierre (1962) The Aim and Structure of Physical Theory. New York:

Ellis, George, F.R. Progress in Scientific and Spiritual Understanding, Spiritual Information 100 Perspectives on Science and Religion, Charles L. Harper, Jr. ed. Philadelphia, PA: Templeton Foundation Press, 2005, pp. 130-131.

Emery, F. E. (1967). The Next Thirty Tears: Concepts, Methods and Anticipations. Human Relations 20(3), pp.199-237.

Emery, F. E. & Trist, E. L. (1960). Socio-Technical Systems. Management Science Models and Techniques, vol. 2. Churchman and Verhulst (Eds.). Oxford: Pergamon.

Emery, F. E. & Trist, E. L. (1973). Towards a Social Ecology:Appreciations of the Future in the Present. New York: Plenum.

Fals-Borda, O. Rahman, M.A. (1991) Action and Knowledge: Breaking the Monopoly with Participatory Action Research. Apex Press: New York.

Fensel, Dieter & Siorpaes, Katharina (2010): Intelligent Systems.

Fereidunian, Alireza e al: A Complex Adaptive System of Systems Approach to Human–Automation Interaction in Smart Grid. Smart Grid Lab, Faculty of Electrical Engineering, K. N. Toosi University of Technology,

Feyerabend, Paul (1993). Against Method, Third Edition. New York: Verso.

Flood, Robert L. (1989a). Archaeology of Systems Inquiry. Systems Practice., 2, 117-124.

Flood, Robert L. (1989b). Six Scenarios for the Future of Systems "Problem Solving". Systems Practice., 2, 75-99.

Flood, Robert L. (1990) Liberating Systems Theory. Plenum New York.

Flood, Robert L. (1993) Beyond TQM. Wiley: New York.

Flood, Robert L; Jackson, Michael C. (1991) Critical Systems Thinking: Directed Readings. Wiley: Chichester.

Flood, Robert L.; Romm, Norma R. A. (1995a). Diversity Management: Theory in Action. Systems Practice, 8(4), 469.

Flood, Robert L: Romm, Norma R. A. (1995b) Enhancing the Process of Methodology Choice in Total Systems Intervention (TSI) and Improving Chances of Tackling Coercion. Systems Practice, 8(4), 377.

Flood, Robert L., Romm, Norma R. A. (1996): Critical Systems Thinking: Current Research and Practice. Plenum: New York & London.

Florian, M. (1974). On the Teaching of Model Building: Mathematical Techniques and Data Analysis.

Friedman, Michael (1974) "Explanation and Scientific Understanding." Journal of Philosophy 71: 5-19.

Gabriel, Henmar (1990). Tools and Techniques of Project Management. Tucson, AZ: Probity Corp.

Gadamer, Hans-Georg (1975). Truth and Method. London: Sheed and Ward.

Galbraith, Jay (1973). Designing Complex Organizations. Reading, MA: Addison-Wesley Publishing Company.

Gardiner (Ed.), Theories of History: Readings from Classical and Contemporary Sources, New York: Free Press, pp. 443-475

Gasparski, Wojciech (1984). Understanding Design:The Praxeological–Systemic Perspective. Seaside, CA: Intersystems Publications.

Georgiou, Ion (2007) Thinking Through Systems Thinking. Routledge: London.

Glasersfeld, Ernst von (1995) Radical Constructivism: A Way of Knowing and Learning. Falmer Press: London.

Gleiser, Marcelo (2005). Emergent Realities in the Cosmos, Spiritual Information: 100 Perspectives on Science and Religion, Charles L. Harper, Jr. ed. Philadelphia, PA: Templeton Foundation Press, 2005.

Goguen, Tad (1986). Designing Learning Systems for Anxiety Management in Clinical Training Systems. San Francisco: Saybrook Institute (Unpublished Essay).

Goodenough, Ursula (1998). The Sacred Depths of Nature, New York, New York: Oxford Universitry Press.

Goodman, Nelson (1978). Ways of Worldmaking. Indianapolis, IN: Hackett Publishing.

Gorin Yu. (1973). A Guide to Physical Effects for Solving Inventive Problems, Baku, (in Russian: Ю.Горин. Указатель Физических Эффектов для Решения Изобретательских Задач, Баку, 1973)

Green, Sara & Wolkenhauer, Olaf (2017). Tracing Organizing Principles: Learning from the His tory of Systems Biology. Stellenbosch Institute for Advanced Study (STIAS) Wallenberg Research Centre Stellenbosch University Marais Road, Stellenbosch, South Africa.

Gregory, Wendy J. Ph.D. (1992) Critical Systems Thinking and Pluralism: A New Constellation. Systems Science Department, The City University: London.

Gregory, Wendy J. (1996) Dealing with Diversity. In Flood, Robert L. and Romm, Norma R. A., eds. Critical Systems Thinking: Current Research and Practice. Plenum Press: New York, 37–61.

Habermas, Jürgen (1981) The Theory of Communicative Action: Vol. One. Reason and the Rationalization of Society. Polity Press: Cambridge.

Hacking, Ian (1999). The Social Construction of What? Cambridge, Mass: Harvard University Press.

Haidar, Diana, et al. Any Threat: An Opportunistic Knowledge Discovery Approach to Insider Threat Detection. December 4, 2018.

Halkes, Catherina. Feminism and Spirituality, Spirituality Today, Autumn 1988, Vol. 40 No. 3, pp. 220-236.

Hardon, John A., S.J. Contemporary Spirituality, Father John A. Hardon Archives, Conference Transcription from a Retreat. (1988). Inter Mirifica. The Real Presence Association, Inc. 7030 West 63rd Street, Chicago: Ill.

Harman, Gilbert (1965) "The Inference to the Best Explanation." Philosophical Review, 74: 88-95.

Harper, Charles, Jr. (ED.) (2005). Spiritual Information. Templeton Foundation Press, Philadelphia.

G. Randolph Mayes Email: mayesgr@csus.edu California State University Sacramento U. S. A. (1986a).

Held, David (1980). Introduction to Critical Theory: Horkheimer to Habermas. Berkeley: University of California Press.

Hempel, Carl G. and Oppenheim, Paul (1948) "Studies in the Logic of Explanation." In Brody p. 8-38.

Hempel, Carl G. (1965) Aspects of Scientific Explanation and other Essays in the Philosophy of Science. New York: Free Press.

Hodge, Richard. A Systems Approach to Strategy and Execution in National Security Enterprises. (PhD THESIS). Defence and Systems Institute, University of South Australia. 31 January 2010

Holland, John; Holyoak, Keith; Nisbett, Richard; Thagard, Paul (1986) Induction: Processes of Inference, Learning, and Discovery. Cambridge: MIT Press

Holt, Bradley P. (2005). Thirsty for God A Brief History of Christian Spirituality. Minneapolis, MINN: Fortress Press.

Hume, David (1977) An Enquiry Concerning Human Understanding. Indianapolis: Hackett

Hutchings, Alice, Clayton, Richard & Anderson, Ross: Taking Down Websites to Prevent Crime (2016). Computer Laboratory, University of Cambridge, Cambridge CB3 0FD

Huyssteen, J. Wentzel Van (2006). Alone in the World? Human Uniqueness in Science and Theology. William B. Eerdmans Publishing Company: Grand Rapids, Michigan.

Idinopulos, Thomas A. (1971). The Erosion of Faith an Inquiry Into the Origins of the Contemporary Crisis in Religious Thought. Quadrangle Books Inc., Chicago, Ill.

Ingvar, David (1985). Memory of the Future:An Essay on the Temporal Organization of Conscious Awareness, Human Neurobiol, 1985; 4: 127-36.

Ivanov, Kristo (1989b). Computer Applications and Organizational Disease. The Well-Being of Organizations, C. West Churchman (Editor). pp. 283-312. Salinas, CA: Intersystems Publications.

Ivanov, Kristo (1989c). Information Systems Design through Creativity: A Tutorial Route Towards Aesthetics and Ethics. Umea, Sweden: University of Umea: Institute of Information Processing Department of Administrative Data Processing.

Ivanov, Kristo (1990). Hypersystems: A Base for Specification of Computer-Supported Self-Learning Social Systems. Umea, Sweden: University of Umea: Institute of Information Processing Administrative Data Processing.

Ivanov, Kristo (1991a). Computer-Supported Human Science or Humanistic Computing Science? Steps Toward the Evaluation of a Humanistic Computing Science. Umea, Sweden: University of Umea: Institute of Information Processing Administrative Data Processing.

Ivanov, Kristo (1991b). Computer-Human Interaction as Continuous System Reconstruction. Umea, Sweden: University of Umea, Institute of Information Processing Administrative Data Processing.

Ivanov, Kristo (1991c). Artificial Intelligence in the Context of Cultural Crisis. Umea, Sweden: University of Umea, Institute of Information Processing, Administrative Data Processing.

Ivanov, Kristo (1987). Rule of Law in Information Systems Research: The Role of Ethics in Knowledge-Building Procedures, Especially in the Updating of Inference Networks. Umea, Sweden: Umea University: Institute of Information Processing Administrative Data Processing.

Ivanov, Kristo (1989a). Ideas for Humanistic and Social Science Research about Consequences of the Increasing Use of Information Technology. Umea, Sweden: University of Umea: Institute of Information Processing.

Jackson,M. C.; Keys, P. (1984) Towards a System of Systems Methodologies. Operational Research Society, 35, 473-486.

Jackson, Michael C. (1985) Social Systems Theory and Practice: The Need for a Critical Approach. International Journal of General Systems.10, 135–151.

Jackson, Michael C. (1987). New Directions in Management Science. In Jackson, M. C. & Keys, P., eds. New Directions in Management Science. Gower: Aldershot, 133–164.

Jackson, Michael C. (1997) Pluralism in Systems Thinking and Practice. In Mingers, John C. & Gill, Anthony, eds. Multimethodology: The Theory and Practice of Combining Management Science Methodologies. John Wiley & Sons: Chichester, 347–37 8.

Jackson, Michael C. (1999) Towards Coherent Pluralism in Management Science. Journal of the Operational Research Society, 50, 12-22.

Jackson, Michael C. (2000) Systems Approaches to Management. Kluwer Academic/Plenum: New York, London.

Jaeger, Lydia (2005). Cosmic Order and Divine Word, Spiritual Information: 100 Perspectives on Science and Religion, Charles L. Harper, Jr. ed. Philadelphia, PA: Templeton Foundation Press, 2005.

Jantsch, E. (1976). Evolution and Consciousness. Reading, MA: Addison-Wesley.

Jantsch, E. (1981). The Evolutionary Vision. Boulder, CO: Westview Press.

Jantsch, E. & Waddington, C. H. (1976). Evolution and Consciousness: Human Systems in Transition. Reading, MA: Wiley.

Johnson-Laird, Philip N. (1988). The Computer and the Mind. Cambridge, MA: Harvard University Press.

Jones, Capers (1994). Assessment and Control of Software Risks. Yourdon Press.

Jones, Capers (2010). Software Engineering: Best Practices. McGraw-Hill.

Jones, Capers (2014). The Technical and Social History of Software Engineering. Addison-Wesley (Pearson Education).

Jones, Capers (2016). Software Methodologies, A Quantitative Guide.MathWorks, Inc.

Jones, Capers (2017). Quantifying Software: Global and Industry Perspectives. **Auerbach Publications.**

Jones, Peter H., PhD (2013). Social Systems. OCAD University, Toronto, Canada. Accepted chapter in: Social Systems and Design, Gary Metcalf (editor). Vol. 1 of the Translational Systems Science Series, Springer

Kallas, Endel. Spirituality on this Side of the Atlantic According to Alexis de Tocqueville, Spirituality Today, Winter 1985, Vol. 37, pp. 292-303.

Kaminsky, Donna Marie F. Secular Franciscans: Bearers of Peace, Messengers of Joy, Spirituality Today, Summer 1985, Vol. 37, pp. 120-129.

Kaplan S., Visnepolschi S., Zlotin B. & Zusman, A. (1999). New Tools for Failure and Risk Analysis: An Introduction to Anticipatory Failure Determination (AFD) and The Theory of Scenario Structuring, Ideation International Inc., 1999

Kennan, James, F., S.J. (2004). Moral Wisdom: Lessons and Texts from the Catholic Tradition, Claretian Publications, Quezon City, Philippines

Khomenko N. TRIZ as a General Theory of Powerful Thinking (OTSM), collection of articles, 1992-2003, http://www.trizminsk.org/e/prs/kho.htm Last seen: 01.12.2013.

Kilpatrick, William (2012). Christianity, Islam, and Atheism: The Struggle for the Soul of the West. Ignatius Press, San Francisco

Kitcher, Philip (1981) "Explanatory Unification." Philosophy of Science 48:507-531.

Klir, G. (1985). Architecture of Systems Problem Solving. New York: Plenum Press.

Klubertanz, George P., S. J. (1953). The Philosophy of Human Nature. New York: Appleton-Century Crofts, Inc.

Klubertanz, George P., S. J. (1955). Introduction to the Philosophy of Being. Englewood Cliffs: Prentice-Hall, Inc.

Korolyov V.A. Glossary of TRIZ-OTSM Terms. (In Russian: Королёв В.А. Справочник терминов ТРИЗ-ОТСМ. 13 редакция.) http://www.triz.org.ua/enc/ Last seen: 01.12.2013.

Korzybski, Alfred, Science and Sanity: An introduction to Non-Aristotelian Systems and General Semantics, Institute of General Semantics, Lakeville, Conn, 1933.

Kotarbinski, T. (1966). Gnosiology: The Scientific Approach to the Theory of Knowledge. Oxford: Pergamon

Kremer, J. W. (1986). The Human Science Approach as Discourse. The Saybrook Review, 6(1). Spring, pp. 65-106.

Krippner, Stanley, et al. (1985). Toward the Application of General Systems Theory in Humanistic Psychology. Systems Research, 2(2), pp. 105-115. London: International Federation for Systems Research, Pergamon Press Ltd.

Kuhn, T. S. (1970). The Structure of Scientific Revolutions. Chicago: University of Chicago Press.

Kuong, Javier F. (1987). Computer Auditing, Security & Internal Control Manual. Englewood Cliffs: Prentice-Hall, Inc

Land, George & Jarman, Beth (1992). Breakpoint and Beyond: Mastering the Future - Today. New York: Harper Business.

Lane, Byron (1985). Managing People. Sunnyvale, CA: Oasis press.

Langsam, Jude. The Discalced Carmelite Secular Order: One Member's View, Spirituality Today, Summer 1985, Vol. 37, pp. 130-139.

Lantz, Kenneth E. (1986). The Prototyping Methodology. Englewood Cliffs: Prentice-Hall

Laszlo, Ervin (1972a). Introduction to Systems Philosophy. New York: Gordon & Breach; Harper Torchbooks (2nd ed. 1973).

Laszlo, Ervin (1972b). The Systems View of the World. New York: George Braziller.

Lawler, Edward E. III & Rhode, John Grant (1976). Information and Control in Organizations. Pacific Palisades, CA: Goodyear Publishing Company, Inc.

Lecarme, Olivier & Gart, Mireille Pellissier (1986). Software Portability. New York: McGraw-Hill Book Company.

Lehman, M. M. (1980, September). Programs, Life Cycles, and Laws of Software Evolution. Proceedings of the IEEE, 68(9), pp. 1060-1076.

Lehrer, Keith (1990) Theory of Knowledge. Boulder: West View Press.

LeShan, Lawrence, Ph.D. (1990). The Dilemma of Psychology: A Psychologist Looks at His Troubled Profession. New York: Penguin Books.

Levenson, Edgar A. (1972). The Fallacy of Understanding: An Inquiry into the Changing Structure of Psychoanalysis. New York: Basic Books, Inc.

Levin, Ben: (2013) The Simple Art of Governing Complex Systems. University of Toronto,

Levinson, Harry (1972). Organizational Diagnosis. Cambridge: Harvard University Press.

Lewis, David & Greene, James (1982). Thinking Better. New York: Rawson, Wade Publishers.

Lewton, Joel, C. Reformed Spirituality: Towards the Development of a Transcendent Community, Spirituality Today, Autumn 1989, Vol. 41 No. 3, pp. 213-225.

Lightedge (2016): Cyberattack Threat and Prevention: Protecting Your Organization Can Be Easy for You.

Linde, Andrei (2005). Choose Your Own Universe, Spiritual Information 100 Perspectives on Science and Religion, Charles L.

Litterer, Joseph A. (1973). The Analysis of Organizations. New York: John Wiley & Sons.

Litvin S, A. Lyrbomirskiy A., Sigalovskaya I. G3:ID Method Glossary. (In Russian: С.Литвин, А.Любомирский, И.Сигаловская. Глоссарий к методике G3:ID.) http://gen3.ru/ru/3605/5453/. Last seen: 01.12.2013.

Litvin S., Lyobomirskiy A. Laws of Engineering Systems Evolution (In Russian: Законы развития технических систем. А.Любомирский, С.Литвин.)

Litvin S., Petrov V., Rubin M., (2007). TRIZ Body of Knowledge.

Lobel, Jerome (1986). Foiling the System Breakers: Computer Security and Access Control. New York: McGraw-Hill Book Company.

Lundell, Jay & Notess, Mark (1991). Human Factors in Software Development: Models, Techniques, and Outcomes. Human Factors in Computing Systems: Reaching through Technology, CHI '91 Conference Proceedings. Robertson, Scott P., Olson, Gary M., & Olson, Judith (Eds.). April-May, pp. 145-152. New Orleans, LA: ACM SIGCHI.

Lundy, James L. (1991). Lead, Follow, or Get Out of the Way: Invaluable Insights into Leadership Style. Quezon City, Philippines: Kadena Press, University of the Philippines.

Maccoby, Michael (1988). Why Work: Motivating and Leading the New Generation. New York: Simon & Schuster.

Mackintosh, Hugh Ross (1937). Types of Modern Theology. New York, New York: Scribner's.

Macnaughton, Ian (1987). Design in the Context of Human Activity Systems. San Francisco: Saybrook Institute (Unpublished Essay).

Madala, S. & Sinclair, J. B. (1991, January). Performance of Synchronous Parallel Algorithms with Regular Structures. IEEE Transactions on Parallel and Distributed Systems, 2(1). Washington, D.C: IEEE Computer Society.

Magnin, Thierry (2005). Quantum Logic and the God-World Relationship: A New Resource for Exploring Modern Christian Theology, Spiritual Information: 100 Perspectives on Science and Religion, Charles L. Harper, Jr. ed. Philadelphia, PA: Templeton Foundation Press.

Mair, William C., Wood, Donald R., & Davis, Keagle W. (1972). Computer Control & Audit. Wellesley, MA: Q.E.D. Information Sciences, Inc.

Management Research Group (1983). Management Effectiveness Analysis. Portland, ME: Management Research Group.

Management Research Group (1987). Leadership Effectiveness Analysis: An Introductory Guide. Portland, ME: Management Research Group.

Manzini, Andrew O. (1988). Organizational Diagnosis: A Practical Approach to Company Problem Solving and Growth. New York: American Management Association.

Manzini, Andrew O. & Gridley, John. (1986). Integrating Human Resources and Strategic Business Planning. New York: American Management Association.

Maritain, Jacque (1952). Range of Reason. New York: Charles Scribner & Sons.

Martel, Leon (1986). Mastering Change: The Key to Business Success. London: Grafton Books.

Martin, James (1973). Security, Accuracy and Privacy in Computer Systems. Englewood Cliffs: Prentice-Hall, Inc.

Martin, James (1984). An Information Systems Manifesto. Englewood Cliffs: Prentice-Hall,

Martin, James (1985a). System Design from Provably Correct Constructs. Englewood Cliffs: Prentice-Hall, Inc.

Martin, James & McClure, Carma (1983). Software Maintenance: The Problem and Its Solutions. Englewood Cliffs: Prentice-Hall, Inc.

Martin, James & McClure, Carma (1988). Structured Techniques: The Basis of CASE. Englewood Cliffs: Prentice-Hall, Inc.

Martin, James & Oxman, Steven (1988). Building Expert Systems: A Tutorial. Englewood Cliffs: Prentice-Hall, Inc.

Marty, Martin E. If Theologians Do Not Measure, Can They Measure Up? Rules For Acquiring Spiritual Information, Spiritual Information 100 Perspectives on Science and Religion, Charles L. Harper, Jr. ed. Philadelphia, PA: Templeton Foundation Press, 2005, pp. 473-478.

Mattessich, Richard (1982). The Systems Approach: Its Variety of Aspects. Journal of the American Society for Information Science.

Maturana, Humberto R. (1988). Ontology of Observing: The Biological Foundations of Self-Consciousness.

Matvienko N.N. TRIZ Terms (Problem Collection). (In Russian: Матвиенко Н.Н. Термины ТРИЗ (проблемный сборник). http://www.metodolog.ru/node/689. Last seen: 01.12.2013.

Mayer, Michael (1984). The Mystery of Personal Identity. San Diego: ACS Publications, Inc.

McCabe, Thomas J. (1980). Software Quality Assurance: A Survey. Columbia, MD: McCabe & Associates.

McClelland, James L., Rumelhart, David E. & The PDP Research Group (1986). Parallel Distributed Processing: Explorations in the Microstructures of Cognition, Volume 2: Psychological and Biological Models. Cambridge, MA: The MIT Press.

McGinn, Bernard (2005). The Letter and the Spirit: Spirituality as an Academic Discipline, in Mind the Spirit: The Study of Christian Spirituality. Elizabeth A. Dreyer & Mark S. Burrows (Eds.). Baltimore, MD: The Johns Hopkins University Press. pp. 25-41.

McKie, James W. (Ed.) (1974). Social Responsibility and the Business Predicament. Washington, D.C: The Brookings Institution.

McLean (1976). The Human Side of Systems: The User's Perspective. Presented at the Western Systems Conference. Los Angeles.

McMillan, Grant R., et al. (1989). Applications of Human Performance Models to System Design. New York: Plenum Press.

McNicholas, James B. III & Houssain Kettani (2019). Consideration of Insider Based Collusion Attacks on Cyber Systems.

Mercer, Michael W. (1989). Turning Your Human Resources Department Into a Profit Center. New York: AMACOM.

Merker, S. L. (1985). Living Systems Theory: A Framework for Management. Behavioral Science, 30, pp. 187-194.

Merker, S. L. (1986). Living Systems Process Analysis in the Far-East: A Review of Two Studies. Proceedings of the Society for General Systems Research, 1, G., pp. 42-51.

Metzger, Philip W. (1987). Managing Programming People: A Personal View. Englewood Cliffs: Prentice-Hall, Inc

McManus, Sonia, et al., (2017). Resilience Management: A Framework for Assessing and Improving the Resilience of Organizations. Resilient Organizations Research Report 2007/01 New Zealand

Midgley, Gerald (1989). Critical Systems: The Theory and Practice of Partitioning Methodologies. Proceedings of the 33rd Annual Meeting of the International Society for General Systems Research. Edinburgh.

Midgley, Gerald (1992). Pluralism and the Legitimation of Systems Science. Systems Practice, 5(2), 147-172.

Midgley, Gerald (1996). What Is This Thing Called CST? Flood, Robert. L. and Romm, N. R. A., eds. Critical Systems Thinking: Current Research and Practice. Plenum: New York, 11–24.

Midgley, Gerald (2000). Systemic Intervention: Philosophy, Methodology, and Practice. Kluwer Academic/Plenum: New York.

Midgley, Gerald (2011). Theoretical Pluralism in Systemic Action Research. Systems Practice and Action Research, 24(1), 1–15.

Miller, Eric (Ed.). (1991). Future Vision: The 189 Most Important Trends of the 1990s. Naperville, IL: Sourcebooks Trade.

Miller, G. A. (1978). The Magical Number Seven, Plus or Minus Two: Some Limits in Our Capacity for Processing Information. Psychology Review, 63(2), pp. 81-97.

Miller, J. G. (1978). Living Systems. New York: McGraw-Hill Book Company.

Miller, J. G. & Miller, J. L. (1980). The Family as a System. C. Hofling and J. Lewis (Eds.), The Family: Evaluation and Treatment, pp. 141-184, New York: runner/Mazel.

Miller, J. G. & Miller, J. L. (1989). A General Living Systems Analysis of Organizational Pathology. The Well-Being of Organizations, C. West Churchman (Ed.). Salinas, CA: Intersystems Publications.

Mills, D. Quinn (1991). Rebirth of the Corporation. New York: John Wiley & Sons, Inc.

Mingers, John C. (2000). The Contribution of Critical Realism as an Underpinning Philosophy for OR/MS and Systems. Journal of the Operational Research Society, 51(11), 12561270.

Mingers, John C. (2003). A Classification of the Philosophical Assumptions of Management Science Methods. Journal of the Operational Research Society, 54(6), 559-570 doi: 10.1057/palgrave.jors. 2601436|ISSN 0160-5682.

Mingers, John C. (2006). Realising Systems Thinking: Knowledge and Action in Management Science. Springer: New York.

Mishkoff, Henry C. (1985). Understanding Artificial Intelligence. Dallas: Texas Instruments.

Mitroff, I. I. & Kilmann, R. H. (1978). Methodological Approaches to Social Sciences. San Francisco: Jossey-Bass.

Mohrman, Susan Albers & Cummings, Thomas G. (1989). Self-Designing Organizations: Learning How to Create High Performance. Menlo Park, CA: Addison-Wesley Publishing Company.

Montalbano, Michael (1974). Decisions Tables. Chicago: Science Research Associates, Inc

Montazemi, Ali Reza & Gupta Kalyan Moy (2006): A Framework for Retrieval in Case-Based Reasoning Systems. School of Business, McMaster University, Hamilton, Ontario, Canada L8S 4M4

Montelibano, Joji & Andrew Moore (2012): Insider Threat Security Reference Architecture.

Morgan, Gareth (1986). Images of Organization. Sage: London.

Mowshowitz, A. (1976). The Conquest of Will: Information Processing in Human Affairs. Reading, MA: Addison-Wesley.

Muftic, Sead (1989). Security Mechanisms for Computer Networks. New York: Halstead Press, a Division of John Wiley & Sons.

Mulligan, Robert W., S. J. (1952). Truth: A Translation of Quaestiones Disputatae Deveritate, Questions I-IX of St. Thomas Aquinas. Chicago: Henry Regnery Company.

Murdoch, Iris (1992). Metaphysics as a Guide to Morals. New York, New York: The Penguin Press.

Murphy, Michael A. & Parker, Xenia Ley (1989). Handbook of EDP Auditing. Boston: Warren, Gorham & Lamont, Inc.

Murphy, Nancey, C. (2005). The Role of Discernment in Seeking Spiritual Knowledge, Spiritual Information: 100 Perspectives on Science and Religion, Charles L. Harper, Jr. ed. Philadelphia, PA: Templeton Foundation Press, 2005.

Musa, Iannino & Okumoto (1987). Software Reliability: Measurement, Prediction, and Application. New York: McGraw-Hill, Inc.

Myers, Glendord J. (1975). Reliable Software through Composite Design. New York: Van Nostrand Reinhold Company.

Myers, Glendord J. (1976). Software Reliability. New York: John Wiley & Sons.

Nadel, Robert B. (1987). Avoiding Micro-Computer Headaches: How to Control the Acquisition, Use, and Security Risks of Microcomputers. New York: McGraw-Hill Book Company.

Nadler, David A. (1977). Feedback and Organization Development: Using Data-Based Methods. Reading, MA: Addison-Wesley Publishing Company.

Nadler, Gerald (1967). Work Systems Design: The Ideals Concept. Homewood, IL: Richard D. Irwin, Inc.

Nadler, Gerald (1987). An Assessment of Systems Methodology and Design. B. H. Banathy (Ed.), Systems Inquiry, pp. 114-123. Louisville, KY: Society for General Systems Research.

Nadler, Gerald & Hibino, Shozo (1990). Breakthrough Thinking: Why We Must Change the Way We Solve Problems, and the Seven Principles to Achieve This. Rocklin, CA: Prima Publishing & Communications.

National Computer Security Center (1985). Personal Computer Security Considerations. Washington, D.C: National Computer Security Center.

National Computer Security Center (1988). Glossary of Computer Security Terms. Washington, D.C: National Computer Security Center.

Naughton, J. (1977). The Checkland Methodology: A Readers Guide, Second Edition. Milton Keynes: Open University Press.

Nemoto, Masao (1987). Total Quality Control for Management: Strategies and Techniques from Toyota and Toyoda Gosei. Englewood Cliffs: Prentice-Hall, Inc.

Newkirk, Raymond L. (1976). The Descent of Man. New York: NYIT.

Newkirk, Raymond L. (1979). Preliminary Phased Development Process Plan. Fort Lauderdale, FL: Systems Engineering Laboratories.

Newkirk, Raymond L. (1981a). Preliminary Phased Documentation: An Overview. Fort Lauderdale, FL: Systems Engineering Laboratories.

Newkirk, Raymond L. (1981b). Phased Documentation Process: An Overview. Fort Lauderdale, FL: Systems Engineering Laboratories.

Newkirk, Raymond L. (1982). The Chronicles of the Making of a Philosopher: Book I: What is Philosophy? Fort Lauderdale, FL: Columbia Pacific University, (Master Thesis).

. **Newkirk, Raymond L.** (1982). The Chronicles of the Making of a Philosopher: Book II: Metaphysicas is Life in Motion. Fort Lauderdale, FL: Columbia Pacific University.

Newkirk, Raymond L. (1982). The Chronicles of the Making of a Philosopher: Book III: Theocity and the Human Spirit. Fort Lauderdale, FL: Columbia Pacific University,

Newkirk, Raymond L. (1982). The Chronicles of the Making of a Philosopher: Book IV: Mother Philosophy, Love of the Ages? Fort Lauderdale, FL: Columbia Pacific University,

Newkirk, Raymond L. (1982). The Chronicles of the Making of a Philosopher: Book V, Part 1, In Defense of Reason, Fort Lauderdale, FL: Columbia Pacific University.

Newkirk, Raymond L. (1982). The Chronicles of the Making of a Philosopher: Book V, Part II, In Defense of Reason, Fort Lauderdale, FL: Columbia Pacific University.

Newkirk, Raymond L. (1984a). Phased Development Process: An Overview. Jeddah, KSA: Royal Saudi Naval Forces.

Newkirk, Raymond L. (1984b). Project "A" Documentation Enhancement Plan. Jeddah, KSA: Royal Saudi Naval Forces (RSNF).

Newkirk, Raymond L. (1984c). The Process Philosophy of Project "A". Jeddah, KSA: RSNF.

Newkirk, Raymond L. & Reynolds, Michael L. (1984a). Phased Development Process: Project "A" Master Schedule. Jeddah, KSA: Royal Saudi Naval Forces.

Newkirk, Raymond L. & Reynolds, Michael L. (1984b). Phased Development Process: Project "A" Project Management Plan the Naval Supply Center Phased Automated Process. Jeddah, KSA: Royal Saudi Naval Forces.

Newkirk, Raymond L. & Reynolds, Michael L. (1984c). Phased Development Process: An Overview of the Project "A" Procedures Management Systems. Jeddah, KSA: RSNF.

Newkirk, Raymond L. & Reynolds, Michael L. (1984d). Phased Development Process: Project "A" Master Plan. Jeddah, KSA: Royal Saudi Naval Forces.

Newkirk, Raymond L. (1985a). Implementation Planning for Information Center Management, Vol.1. Quezon City, Philippine Islands: International Association for Information Management.

Newkirk, Raymond L. (1985b). Implementation Planning for Information Center Management, Vol. 2. Quezon City, Philippine Islands: International Association for Information Management.

Newkirk, Raymond L. (1985c). Phased Development Process Project "L" the Long-Range Plan for AFP: Automated Integrated Logistics Systems. Manila: IAIM.

Newkirk, Raymond L. (1986a). Post Implementation Review Handbook. Pleasant Hill, CA:

(Pacific Bell MTS Project Document).

Newkirk, Raymond L. (1986b). Gestalt Training Process: Phased Training Plan Guidelines for Water and Sewer Customer Information and Billing System. San Francisco: IAIM.

Newkirk, Raymond L. (1987a). Post Implementation Review Handbook for Pacific Bell. San Ramon, CA: International Association of Information Management Press.

Newkirk, Raymond L. (1987b). A Systems Models Description of a Software Development System. San Francisco: Saybrook Institute.

Newkirk, Raymond L. (1988a). Operations Management in the 1990's. Pleasant Hill, CA: SMI.

Newkirk, Raymond L. (1988b). A Deductive Process Model of the Computer Software Development Human Activity System. Pleasant Hill, CA: Saybrook Institute.

Newkirk, Raymond L. (1988c). An LSPA Description of the Computer Software Development Human Activity System. San Francisco: Saybrook Institute.

Newkirk, Raymond L. (1988d). An Emerging Redesign of the Computer Software Development Human Activity System Using Living Systems Theory Guided by the Systems Models Approach. San Francisco: Saybrook Institute.

Newkirk, Raymond L. (1988e). Three Alternative Root Definitions of the Computer Software Development Human Activity System. San Francisco: Saybrook Institute

Newkirk, Raymond L. (1988f). A Conceptual Model of a Problem Situation Existing in the Software Development Human Activity System. San Francisco: Saybrook Institute

Newkirk, Raymond L. (1988g). A Project Proposal for the Design of a Computer Software Development Human Activity System. San Francisco: Saybrook Institute.

Newkirk, Raymond L. (1988h). The Nature and Characterization of Human Activity Systems in General and the Computer Software Development Human Activity System in Particular. San Francisco: Saybrook Institute.

Newkirk, Raymond L. (1988i). A Description of the Software Development Human Activity System. San Francisco: Saybrook Institute.

Newkirk, Raymond L. (1988j). A Comprehensive Characterization and Description of the Software Development Human Activity System. San Francisco: Saybrook Institute.

Newkirk, Raymond L. (1988k). Integrating Human Resource Planning with the Information Technology Business Plan: The Path to Contingency Planning. Pleasant Hill, CA: SMI.

Newkirk, Raymond L. (1989a). Capacity Management of the Corporate Computer System. Pleasant Hill, CA: Systems Management Institute Press.

Newkirk, Raymond L. (1989b). The Living Systems Approach: A New Software Design Paradigm for the 21st Century and Beyond. Pleasant Hill, CA: Saybrook Institute.

Newkirk, Raymond L. (1989c). Software Quality Assurance and Control. Pleasant-Hill, CA: Systems Management Institute.

Newkirk, Raymond L. (1989d). Design Operations and Tasks Leading to the Redesign of the Computer Software Development Human Activity System. San Francisco: Saybrook Institute.

Newkirk, Raymond L (1989e). The Design System Supporting the Redesign of the Computer Software Development Human Activity System. San Francisco: Saybrook Institute.

Newkirk, Raymond L. (1989f). Developmental Objectives and Plans Supporting the Redesign of the Computer Software Development Human Activity System. San Francisco: Saybrook Institute.

Newkirk, Raymond L. (1989g). The Living Systems Approach a New Software Design Paradigm for the 21st Century and Beyond. San Francisco: Saybrook Institute.

Newkirk, Raymond L. (1989h). Revised Approach for the Design of the Software Development Human Activity System. San Francisco: Saybrook Institute.

Newkirk, Raymond L. (1989i). A Review of the Traditional Approach to Computer Software Development – An Ideology Critique. San Francisco: Saybrook Institute.

Newkirk, Raymond L. (1989j). The Creativity Myth: A New Software Design Paradigm for the 21st Century and Beyond. San Francisco: Saybrook Institute.

Newkirk, Raymond L. (1990a). SPAC Real Time Processing System Operational Evaluation Audit Handbook, Vol. I. Pleasant Hill, CA: Systems Management Institute Press.

Newkirk, Raymond L. (1990b). SPAC Real Time Processing System Operational Evaluation Audit Handbook, Vol.II. Pleasant Hill, CA: Systems Management Institute Press.

Newkirk, Raymond L. (1990c). Design Evaluation and Measurement: Evolutionary Guidance. System, San Francisco: Saybrook Institute.

Newkirk, Raymond L. (1990d). Executive Information Systems: Foundation for Tomorrow. Pleasant Hill, CA: Systems Management Institute.

Newkirk, Raymond L. (1990e). The Design of the Software Development Group as a Systems Issue. San Francisco: Saybrook Institute.

Newkirk, Raymond L. (1990f). A Research Proposal for the Redesign of the Software Quality and Control Group. San Francisco: Saybrook Institute.

Newkirk, Raymond L. (1991a). Metamethodology Design Foundation for Tomorrow. Pleasant Hill, CA: Systems Management Institute.

Newkirk, Raymond L. (1991b). Philosophical Foundation of a Metamethodology for Design Inquiry in Software Development Human Activity Systems. San Francisco, CA: Saybrook.

Newkirk, Raymond L. (1992). Using the Human Systems Methodology to Design the Strategic Organization. Concord, CA: Systems Management Institute (Seminar Presentation).

Newkirk, Raymond L. (1999). Beyond the Year 2000 Crisis, Systems Management Institute Press, Pleasant Hill, CA

Newkirk, Raymond L. (2006). Leading By Design. Booklocker, FL

Newkirk, Raymond L. (2019). The Benefits of Human-Centered Insider Threat Prevention. Systems Management Institute Press. Orlando. FL.

Niebling, Carl & Christie, Marian (1991). Competitive Behavior. Wassenaar, The Netherlands: Niebling Productions.

NIST (2018). Cybersecurity is Everyone's Job. Publication of the National Initiative for Cybersecurity Education Working Group: Subgroup on Workforce Management at the National Institute of Standards and Technology.

Norman, Maxwell H. (1974). Dimensions of the Future Alternatives for Tomorrow. New York: Holt, Rinehart and Winston, Inc.

O'Connell, Patrick, F. St Francis of Assisi: The Spirituality of Conformation, Spirituality Today, Winder 1986, Vol. 38, pp. 1-11.

Offerman, Lynn R. & Growing, Marilyn K. (1990, February). Organizations of the Future: Changes and Challenges. American Psychologist, 45(2), pp. 95-108.

Ohmae, Kenichi (1990). The Borderless World: Power and Strategy in the Interlinked Economy. New York: Harper Business, Harper Collins Publishers.

Oldham, John M., M.D. & Morris, Lois B. (1990). Personality Self-Portrait: Why You Think, Work, Love, and Act the Way You Do. New York: Bantam Books.

Olle, Hagelstein, et al. (1988). Information Systems Methodologies: A Framework for Understanding. Menlo Park, CA: Addison-Wesley Publishing Company.

Ormerod, R.J (2008). The Transformation Competence Perspective. University of Warwick, Coventry, UK

Orr, Ken (1977). Structured Systems Development. Yourdon Press.

Orr, Ken (1981). Structured Requirements Definition. Ken Orr, Publisher, Kansas

Orr, Ken (2984). The One Minute Methodology. Optima Inc.

Oskamp, Stuart (1990). Overconfidence in Case-Study Judgments. Judgment Under Uncertainty: Heuristics and Biases. Kahneman, Slovic & Tversky (Eds.), Cambridge, England: Cambridge University Press.

Ouellette, L. Paul (1992). How to Market the I/S Department Internally: Gaining the Recognition & Strategic Position You Merit. New York: AMACOM.

Overton, Willis F. (1975). General Systems, Structure, and Development. Structure and Transformation: Developmental and Historical Aspects, Volume 3., Chapter 4. John Wiley & Sons., Inc.

Overton, Willis F. & Ennis, Michelle D. (2006). Cognitive-Developmental and Behavioral-Analytic Theories: Evolving into Complementarity. Journal of Human Develoipment.Temple University

Pagels, Heinz (1988). The Dreams of Reason: The Computer and the Rise of the Sciences of Complexity. New York: Simon and Schuster.

Pandikattu, Kuruvilla (2005). Spiritual Information for Integral Transformation, Spiritual Information 100 Perspectives on Science and Religion, Charles L. Harper, Jr. ed. Philadelphia, PA: Templeton Foundation Press.

Parberry, Ian (1987). Parallel Complexity Theory. New York: John Wiley & Sons.

Parentchik G.I. (2013). Terminological Aspect of TRIZ. (In Russian: Паренчик Г.И. Терминологический Аспект ТРИЗ). http://www.metodolog.ru/00252/00252.html Last seen: 01.12.2013.

Parikh, Girisj (1982). How to Measure Programmer Productivity. Wellesley, MA: Q.E.D. Information Sciences, Inc.

Parker, D. B. (1976). Crime by Computer. New York: Scribner's.

Parker, Nycum & Oura (1973). Computer Abuse. Washington, D. C: National Technical Information Service.

Pascale, Richard Tanner (1990). Managing on the Edge: How the Smartest Companies Use Conflict to Stay Ahead New York: Simon and Schuster.

Pasmore, William A. (1988). Designing Effective Organizations: The Sociotechnical Systems Perspective. New York: John Wiley & Sons.

Pava, C. (1983). Managing New Office Technology: An Organizational Strategy. New York: The Free Press.

Pelikan, Jaroslav, and Lehmann, Helmut T. eds. Luther's Works, 56 vols. St. Louis: Concordia Publishing House. Philadelphia: Fortress Press, 1955: 37:228.

Penzias, Arno (1989). IDEAS and Information. New York: Simon Schuster, Inc.

Perlmutter, H. (1965). Towards a Theory and Practice of Human Architecture. London: Tavistock.

Perls, Frederick S. (1971). Gestalt Therapy Verbatim. New York: Bantam Books.

Perry, D. E. & Kaiser, G. E. (1991, March). Models of Software Development Environments. IEEE Transactions on Software Engineering,17(3). College Park, MD: IEEE Computer Society.

Perry, William (1986). A Standard for Auditing Computer Applications: Selected Audit Areas. Pennsauken, NJ: Auerbach Publishers, Inc.

Perry, William (1986). A Standard for Auditing Computer Applications: Auditing Microcomputer Systems. Pennsauken, NJ: Auerbach Publishers, Inc.

Perry, William (1986). Cleaning Up a Computer Mess: A Guide to Diagnosing and Correcting Computer Problems. New York: Van Nostrand Reinhold Company.

Perry, William (1987). A Standard for Testing Applications Software: Testing Computer Security. Boston: Auerbach Publishers, Inc.

Peters, Tom (1987). Thriving on Chaos: The Handbook for a Management Revolution. New York: Alfred A. Knopf.

Peters, Tom (1993). Liberation Management. New York: Random House.

Peters, Tom & Waterman, Robert H., Jr. (1982). In Search of Excellence. New York: Alfred A. Knopf.

Peters, Tom & Austin, Nancy (1983). A Passion for Excellence. New York: Alfred A. Knopf.

Peterson, Richard B. & Tracy, Lane (1979). Systematic Management of Human Resources. Reading, MA: Addison-Wesley Publishing Company.

Petrie, H. G. (1968). The Strategy Sense of Methodology. Philosophy of Science, pp. 248-257.

Petrov V. (2006). Law – Antilaw. ETRIA TRIZ Futures Conference 2006. 5th ETRIA. 9-11 October 2006. Kortrijk, Belgium. pp. 133-140

Petrov V. (2006). History of Developing the Algorithm of Solving Inventive Problems: ARIZ, Tel-Aviv, 2006 (in Russan: В. Петров. История разработки Алгоритма Решения Изобретательских Задач. Тель Авив, 2006).

Petrov V. (2003). History of Developing Standards, Tel-Aviv, 2003 (In Russian: В. Петров. История Развития Стандартов. Тель-Авив, 2003)

Petrov V. (2001). Laws of Systems Evolution, Tel-Aviv, 2001 (In Russian: В. Петров. Законы Развития Систем. Тель-Авив, 2001) http://www.trizland.ru/trizba/books/1759/

Petrov V. (2013). The Laws of System Evolution. Berlin: TriS Europe GmbH, 646 pages (in Russian: INNOVATOR (06) 01/2013, ISSN 1866-4180. Петров В. Законы развития систем. Монография. Тель-Авив, 2013 – 646 с.

Petrov V. (2002). Dictionary of TRIZ Terms, 2002.

Pitt, Joseph C. (1988) Theories of Explanation. Oxford: Oxford University Press.

Polinpapilinho, F. Katina & Ra'ed, M. Jaradat: A Three-Phase Framework for Elicitation of Infrastructure Requirements. International Journal Critical Infrastructures. Vol. 8, Nos. 2/3, 2012. National Centers for System of Systems Engineering, Norfolk, VA 23508, USA

Polinpapilinho F. Katina and Charles B. Keating. Metasystem Pathologies: Towards Discovering of Impediments to System Performance. The National Centers for System of Systems Engineering Department of Engineering Management and Systems Engineering. Old Dominion University, Norfolk, VA Proceedings of the 2016 Industrial and Systems Engineering Research Conference. H. Yang, Z. Kong, and MD Sarder, eds.

Polkinghorne, Donald (1983). Methodology for the Human Sciences: Systems of Inquiry. Albany: State University of New York Press.

Pontifex, Mark & Illtyd, Trethowan (1953). Meaning of Existence. London: Longmans, Green and Company

Posner, Michael I. (ED.) (1989). Foundations of Cognitive Science. Cambridge, MA: MIT Press.

Pouvreau, David (2009). The Dialectical Tragedy of the Concept of Wholeness: Ludwig von Bertalanffy's Biography Revisited. Exploring Unity through Diversity: Volume 1

Pouvreau, David (2013). The Project of "General Systemology" Instigated by Ludwig Von Bertalanffy Genealogy, Genesis, Reception and Advancement. Bertalanffy Center for the Study of Systems Science, Vienna, Austria.

Pouvreau, David (2014). On the History of Ludwig Von Bertalanffy's "General Systemology", and on Its Relationship to Cybernetics - Part II: Contexts and Developments of the Systemological Hermeneutics Instigated by Von Bertalanffy. International Journal of General Systems.

Prevention Committee President's Council on Integrity and Efficiency (1986). Computer: Crimes, Clues and Controls. Washington, D. C: Prevention Committee President's Council on Integrity and Efficiency.

Prigogine, I. (1976). Order through Fluctuation:Self-Organization and Social Systems. Jantsch, E. & Waddington, C. H. (Eds.). Evolution and Consciousness: Human Systems in Transitions. Reading, MA: Addison-Wesley Publishing Company.

Prince, Howard T., II (1985). (Ed.), Leadership in Organizations. West Point: Associates, The Department of Behavioral Science and Leadership, United States Military Academy

Probity, Inc. (1990). Tools and Techniques of Basic Project Management. Tucson: Probity.

Progoff, Ira (1990). Forward, in Mysticism: The Preeminent Study in the Nature and Development of Spiritual Consciousness. Twelfth Edition.Underhill, Evelyn (1990) New York, New York: Doubleday.

Prushinskiy V., Zainiev G. & Gerasimov V. (2005). Hybridization: The New Warfare in the Battle for the Market, Ideation International, Inc., 2005

Pugh, D. S., Hickson, D. J., & Hinings, C. R. (1964). Writers on Structure of Functioning of Management of People in Organizations in Society. New York: Penguin Books.

QED Information Sciences, Inc. (1985a). Security Evaluation for Small Computer Centers. Wellesley, MA: Q.E.D. Information Sciences, Inc.

QED Information Sciences, Inc. (1985b). Disaster Recovery: Contingency Planning and Program Evaluation. Wellesley, MA: Q.E.D. Information Sciences, Inc.

QED Information Sciences, Inc. (1985c). Personnel Productivity Management: Organization, Planning, Implementation and Control. Wellesley, MA: Q.E.D. Information Sciences, Inc.

Quick, James C. & Quick, Jonathan D. (1984). Organizational Stress and Preventive Management. New York: McGraw-Hill Book Company.

Quine, W. V. (1969) "Epistemology Naturalized." In Ontological Relativity and Other Essays. New York: Columbia University Press: 69-90.

Quinn, James Brian (1992). Intelligent Enterprises. New York: The Free Press.

Radner, Daisie & Radner, Michael (1982). Science and Unreason. Belmont, CA: Wadsworth Publishing Company.

Rado, Sandor (1969). Adaptational Psychodynamics: Motivation and Control. New York: Science House.

Rahman, M.A. (1993). People's Self-Development: Perspectives on Participatory Action Research: A Journey through Experience. Zed Books: London.

Ramirez, Rafael, Ph.D. (1991). The Beauty of Social Organization. Munich: ACCEDO Verlagsgesellschaft mbH.

Ramamoorthy, C. V., et al. (1990). The Evolution Support Environment. IEEE

Transactions on Software Engineering,16 (11), pp. 1225-1235.

Ray, Michael and Myers, Rochelle (1986). Creativity in Business. New York: Doubleday.

Reason, P. & Rowan, J. (1981). (Eds.) Human Inquiry: A Sourcebook of New Paradigm Research. Chichester, England: Wiley & Sons.

Reason, P. (ed.) (1988). Human Inquiry in Action: Developments in New Paradigm Research. Sage: London.

Reckmeyer, W. J. (1982). The Emerging Systems Paradigm: A Historical Perspective. Washington, D. C: The American University (Unpublished Doctoral Dissertation).

Ritzer, G. (1977). Working: Conflict and Change. Englewood Cliffs: Prentice-Hall, Inc.

Robertson, Scott P., et al. (1991). Human Factors in Computing Systems: Reaching through Technology, CHI'91 Conference Proceedings. Sponsored by the ACM's SIG on Computer Human Interaction. New York: The Association for Computing Machinery

Robinson, Peter (1991). Real-Time Processing System Presentation. Los Angeles: Security Pacific Automation Company.

Roeber, Richard J. C. (1973). The Organization in a Changing Environment. Reading, MA: Addison- Wesley Publishing Company.

Roethlisberger, F. & Dickson, J. J. (1939). Management and the Worker. Cambridge, MA: Harvard University Press.

Rogers, Joyce. Mysticism as a Way of Spirituality, Spirituality Today, Summer 1988, Vol. 40 No. 2, pp. 100-108.

Rolheiser, Ronald (1999). The Holy Longing: The Search for a Christian Spirituality. Doubleday, New York, New York.

Rorty, Richard (1981). Philosophy and the Mirror of Nature. Princeton, New Jersey: Princeton University Press.

Rorty, Richard (1998). Truth and Progress, Philosophical Papers, Volume 3. New York: Cambridge University Press.

Rosen, Robert H., Ph.D. (1991). The Healthy Company: Eight Strategies to Develop People, Productivity, and Profits. Los Angeles: Jeremy P. Tarcher, Inc.

Rosenau, Pauline Marie (1992). Post-Modernism and the Social Sciences: Insights, Inroads, and Intrusions. Princeton, NJ: Princeton University Press.

Rosenbaum, Stephanie (1989). The Role of Human Factors and Usability Testing in the Software Testing Process. Sixth International Conference on Testing Computer Software, May 25, 1989. Ann Arbor, MI: Tec-Ed Technical Publications and Graphics Services.

Rosenbluth, Hal F. & Peters, Diane McFerrin (1992). The Customer Comes Second and Other Secrets of Exceptional Service. New York: William Morrow and Company, Inc.

Roy, Sonam (2016). Insiders and Insider Threats an Overview of Definitions and Mitigation Techniques. Indian Institute of Space Science and Technology, Thiruvananthapu.

RTPS Operational Evaluation Team (1991). Real Time Processing System (RTPS) Operational Evaluation Analysis. Los Angeles: Security Pacific Automation Company.

RTPS Project Team (1989). Security Pacific Automation Company Real Time Processing System Project High-Level Requirements Document. Los Angeles: SPAC

RTPS Project Team (1990). Security Pacific Automation Company Real Time Processing Project Supplementary. Systems Management Institute, Pleasant Hill, CA.

Ruchlis, Hy & Oddo, Sandra (1990). Clear Thinking: A Practical Introduction. Buffalo: Prometheus Books.

Runes, Dagobert D. (1967). The Treasury of Philosophy. Totowa, NJ: Littlefield, Adams & Company.

Ruscoe, G.C., Fell, R.L., et al. (1985). The Application of Living Systems Theory to 41 U.S. Army Battalions. Behavioral Science, 30, pp. 7-52.

Russell, Jeffrey Burton (2005). Historical Errors Impeding Progress in Science and Religion, Spiritual Information 100 Perspectives on Science and Religion. Charles L. Harper, Jr. (Ed.). Philadelphia, PA: Templeton Foundation Press. pp. 63-67.

Russell, P. (1983). The Global Brain. Los Angeles: J. P. Tarcher.

Russo, J. Edward & Schoemaker, Paul J. H. (1989). Decision Traps: The Ten Barriers to Brilliant Decision-Making and How to Overcome Them. New York: Simon & Schuster, Inc.

Sackman, Harold (1971). Mass Information Utilities and Social Excellence. New York: Auerbach Publishers.

Sakaiya, Taichi (1991). The Knowledge-Value Revolution or a History of the Future. New York: Kodansha International

Salamatov Yu. (1999). TRIZ: The Right Solution at the Right Time. Insytec, The Netherlands, 1999.

Salk, Jonas (1983). Autonomy of Reality: Merging of Intuition and Reason. New York: Columbia University Press.

Salmon, Wesley (1984) Scientific Explanation and the Causal Structure of the World. Princeton: Princeton University Press.

Salmon, Wesley (1990) Four Decades of Scientific Explanation. Minneapolis: University of Minnesota Press.

Salner, Marcia (1985). The Relationship of Naive Epistemology to Formal Epistemology: Implications for the Teaching of Human Science Methodology, Methods, Donald E. Polkinghorne (Ed.). San Francisco: Saybrook Institute.

Sampson, Edward E. (1983). Justice and the Critique of Pure Psychology. New York: Plenum Press.

Savary, Louis M., Berne, Patricia H., & Williams, Strephon Kaplan (1984). Dreams and Spiritual Growth: A Christian Approach to Dreamwork. Ramsey, N.J: Paulist Press.

Schank, Roger & Childers, Peter (1988). The Creative Attitude: Learning to Ask and Answer the Right Questions. New York: Macmillan Publishing Company.

Scharfstein, Ben-Ami, et al. (1978). Philosophy East Philosophy West: A Critical Comparison of Indian, Chinese, Islamic, and European Philosophy. Ben-Ami Scharfstein (Ed.). New York: Oxford University Press

Schloss, Jeffrey, (2005). Hath Darwin Suffered a Prophet's Scorn? Spiritual Information: 100 Perspectives on Science and Religion, Charles L. Harper, Jr. ed. Philadelphia, PA: Templeton Foundation Press, 2005.

Schneiders, Sandra, (2005). The Study of Christian Spirituality: Contours and Dynamics of a Discipline, Minding the Spirit: The Study of Christian Spirituality. Elizabeth A. Dreyer & Marki S. Burrows eds. Baltimore, MD: The Johns Hopkins University Press.

Schneiders, Sandra, (2005). A Hermeneutical Approach to the Study of Christian Spirituality, Minding the Spirit: The Study of Christian Spirituality. Elizabeth A. Dreyer & Marki S. Burrows eds. Baltimore, MD: The Johns Hopkins University Press

Scriven, M (1959) "Truisms as the Grounds for Historical Explanations."

Security Pacific Automation Company (1989a). ADS/Se Software Engineering Methodology. Los Angeles: Security Pacific Automation Company.

Security Pacific Automation Company (1989b). Real-Time Processing System Project High-Level Requirements Document. Los Angeles: Security Pacific Automation Company, RTPS Project Team.

Security Pacific Automation Company (1991). RTPS: Real Time Processing System Operational Evaluation Analysis. Los Angeles: Security Pacific Automation Company.

Sellars, Wilfred (1962) Science, Perception, and Reality. New York: Humanities Press.

Semke, Jeannette & Nurius, Paula (1990, September). Information Structure, Information Technology and the Human Service Organizational Environment. Proceedings of the Conference on Computers and the Quality of Life, CQL '90. Washington, D.C., The George Washington University: ACM Special Interest Group on Computers & Society and ACM Special Interest Group on Computers and the Physically Handicapped, p. 20.

Senge, Peter M. (1990). The Fifth Discipline: The Art & Practice of the Learning Organization. New York: Doubleday.

Shaeffer, Francis (1990). Escape from Reason, in the Francis A. Shaeffer Trilogy. Westchester, IL: Crossway.

Sheldrake, Rupert (1981). A New Science of Life: The Hypothesis of Formative Causation. Los Angeles: Jeremy P. Tarcher, Inc.

Shick, Deana & Kyle O'Meara (2016). A Unique Approach to Threat Analysis Mapping: A Malware-Centric Methodology for Better Understanding, the Adversary Landscape.

Shneiderman, Ben (1991, January). Human Values and the Future of Technology: A Declaration of Responsibility. SIGCHI Bulletin, 23(1). New York: Association for Computing Machinery.

Silberstein, Michael (2005). On the Perennial Oneness of Being, Spiritual Information: 100 Perspectives on Science and Religion, Charles L. Harper, Jr. ed. Philadelphia, PA: Templeton Foundation Press, 2005.

Siler, Todd (1990). Breaking the Mind Barrier. New York: Simon & Schuster.

Silva, Michael & Sjogren, Bertil (1990). Europe 1992 & the New World Power Game. New York: John Wiley & Sons.

Silver, Susan (1989). Organized to Be the Best! Los Angeles: Adams-Hall Publishing.

Simon, Hebert A. (1964). The Architecture of Complexity. Readings in Managerial Psychology, Second Edition. Leavitt, Harold J. & Pondy, Louis R. (Eds.). Chicago: The University of Chicago Press.

Simon, Hebert A. (1969). The Sciences of the Artificial. Cambridge, MA: MIT Press.

Slawski, C. (1987). Causing Social Change. Proceedings of the Society for General Systems Research, Supplement, pp. 66-86.

Sloma, Richard S. (1977). No-Nonsense Management. New York: Bantam Books.

SMI (1990a). Systems Management Institute Audit Team Handbook for the RTPS Operational Evaluation and Performance Test Phase, Vol.1. Pleasant Hill, CA: Systems Management Institute Press.

SMI (1990a). Systems Management Institute Audit Team Handbook for the RTPS Operational Evaluation and Performance Test Phase, Vol. 2. Pleasant Hill, CA: Systems Management Institute Press.

SMI (1990a). Systems Management Institute Audit Team Handbook for the RTPS Operational Evaluation and Performance Test Phase, Vol. 3. Pleasant Hill, CA: SMI Press.

Smith, James K. A. (2006). Who's Afraid of Postmodernism Taking Derrida, Lyotard, and Foucault to Church. Grand Rapids, Michigan: Baker Academic.

Smolarski, Dennis C. (1988). The Spirituality of Computers, Spirituality Today, Winter 1988, Vol. 40 No. 4, pp. 292-307.

Sommer, R. (1974). Tight Spaces: Hard Architecture and How to Humanize It. Englewood Cliffs: Prentice-Hall, Inc

Souchkov V., Kucharavy D., Devoino I. (1991). Invention Machine Terms Dictionary, Invention Machine Labs, 1991.

Spirn, J. R. (1977). Program Behavior: Models and Measurements. New York: Elsevier

Stamps, Jeffrey S. (1980). Holonomy: A Human Systems Theory. Seaside, CA: Intersystems.

Stanat, Ruth (1990). The Intelligent Corporation: Creating a Shared Network for Information and Profit. New York: American Management Association.

Stannard, F. Russell (2005). Proof or Persuasion? Spiritual Information: 100 Perspectves on Science and Religion, Charles L. Harper, Jr. ed. Philadelphia, PA: Templeton Foundation Press, 2005.

Steers, R. M. (1977). Organizational Effectiveness: A Behavioral View. Santa Monica, CA: Goodyear.

Stern, Nancy & Stern, Robert A. (1983). Computers in Society. Englewood Cliffs: Prentice-Hall.

Sternberg, Robert J. (1988). The Triarchic Mind: A New Theory of Human Intelligence. New York: Penguin Books.

Stewart, Hugh B. (1989). Recollecting the Future: A View of Business, Technology, and Innovation in the Next 30 Years. Homewood, IL: Dow Jones-Irwin.

Stich, Stephen P. (Ed.) (1975). Innate Ideas. Berkeley, CA: University of California Press.

Stich, Stephen (1983) From Folk Psychology to Cognitive Science. Cambridge: The MIT Press.

Strauss, Danie (2016). The Tension between (Methodological) Individualism and Holism. Journal of Christian Scholarship.

Studenmund, A. H. (2013). Using Econometrics, Pearson

Suarez, Antoine (2005). Do Quantum Experiments Challenge Kant's Criticism of the Proofs for the Existence of God? Spiritual Information: 100 Perspectives on Science and Religion, Charles L. Harper, Jr. ed. Philadelphia, PA: Templeton Foundation Press, 2005.

Suarez, Francis (1947). On the Various Kinds of Distinctions. Translated by Cyril Vollert in the:Disputationes Metaphysicae, Disp. No. 7. Milwaukee, WI: Marquette University Press

Sutherland, J. W. (1973). A General Systems Philosophy for the Social and Behavioral Sciences. New York: George Braziller.

Taket, Ann & White, Leroy (1996). Pragmatic Pluralism, an Explication. Systems Practice, 9(6), 571-586.

Talbot, Michael (1991). The Holographic Universe. New York: Harper Collins Publishers.

Tapscott, Don & Caston, Art (1993). Paradign Shift the New Promise of Information Technology. New York: McGraw Hill, Inc.

Taylor, Charles (1989). Sources of the Self: The Making of the Modern Identity. Cambridge, MA: Harvard University Press.

Teilhard de Chardin, Pierre (1965). The Phenomenon of Man (2nd ed.). New Your York.

Terninko, John (2011): 40 Inventive Principles with Social Examples. Responsible Management 62 Case Rd. Nottingham, NH 03290-5507 USA

Thagard, Paul (1988) Computational Philosophy of Science. Cambridge: MIT Press.

Thayer, Frederick (1972). General System(s) Theory: The Promise That Could Not Be Kept, Academy of Management Journal, XV (1972).

Thomas, Keith A. (1987). Building an Open System. New York: Van Nostrand Reinhold Company.

Thompson, James D. (1976). Organizations in Action. New York: McGraw-Hill Book Company.

Thompson, John B. (1984). Studies in the Theory of Ideology. Berkeley, CA: University of California Press.

Thomsett, Rob (1993). Third Wave Project Management: A Handbook for Managing the Complex Information Systems for the 1990s. Englewood Cliffs: Prentice Hall, Inc.

Tinbergen, Jan (1958). The Design of Development. The International Development Institute, International Bank for Reconstruction and Development. Baltimore, MD: The Johns Hopkins Press.

Todd, Mary Anne & Guitian, Constance (1989). Computer Security Training Guidelines. Washington, D.C: National Institute of Standards and Technology.

Toffler, A. (1971). Future Shock. New York: Bantam Books.

Toffler, A. (1980). The Third Wave. New York: Bantam Books.

Toffler, A. (1990). Power Shift: Knowledge, Wealth, and Violence at the Edge of the 21st Century. New York: Bantam Books.

Tosi, Henry L. & Hammer, W. Clay (Eds.) (1977). Organizational Behavior and Management: A Contingency Approach. Chicago: St. Clair Press.

Trist, E.L. (1978). Adapting to a Changing World. Readings in Quality of Working Life, George F. Sanderson, (Ed.). Ottawa: Labour Canada, pp. 10-20

Tschudin, Alain J-P. C. (2005). Preparing the Way for the lord: Evolution, Christianity, and the Dialog on Moral Freedom, Spiritual Information: 100 Perspectives on Science and Religion, Charles L. Harper, Jr. ed. Philadelphia, PA: Templeton Foundation Press, 2005.

Tsoukas, Haridimos; Papoulias, Demetrios B. (1996). Creativity in OR/MS: From Technique to Epistemology: Interfaces, 26(2), 73-79.

Turnage, Janet J. (1990, February). The Challenge of New Workplace Technology for Psychology. American Psychologist, 45(2), pp. 171-178.

Ulrich, Werner (1983). Critical Heuristics of Social Planing: A New Approach to Practical Philosophy. Wiley: Chichester.

Underhill, Evelyn (1990). Mysticism: The Preeminent Study in the Nature and Development of Spiritual Consciousness. Twelfth Edition. New York, New York: Doubleday.

Van Fleet, James K. (1983). 25 Steps to Power and Mastery over People. West Nyack, NY: Parker Publishing Company, Inc

van Fraassen, Bas C. (1980) The Scientific Image. Oxford: Clarendon Press.

van Fraassen, Bas C. (1989) Laws and Symmetry. Oxford: Clarendon Press.

Vam Kaam, Adrian, Fr. & Muto, Susan, Dr. (1978). Questions and Answers on Formative Spirituality: Am I Living a Spiritual Life? Dimension Books, New Jersey.

Vetter, Jennifer, (Ed.). (2016). Franciscan Virtues through the Year: 52 Steps to Conversion from St. Francis of Assisi. Written by Members of the Confraternity of Penitents.

Vikentiev I. (1987). A Spatial Geometrical Operator, Leningrad, 1987 (In Russian: И. Викентьев, Пространственный Геометрический Оператор. Ленинград, 1987).

Vost, Kevin (2018). How to Think Like Aquinas. Sophia Institute Press: Manchester, New Hampshire.

Wack, John P. & Carnahan, Lisa A. (1989). Computer Viruses and Related Threats: A Management Guide. Washington, D. C: National Institute of Standards and Technology.

Wadsworth (1973). The Human Side of Data Processing Management. Englewood Cliffs: Prentice-Hall, Inc.

Wagner, Clare (1985). Current Trends: Spirituality in a Dark Age: Some Reflections, Spirituality Today, Spring 1985, Vol. 37, pp. 59-71.

Wallace, Robert H., Stockenberg, John E., & Charette, Robert N. (1987). A Unified

Methodology for Developing Systems. New York: Intertext Publications, Inc., McGraw-Hill, Inc.

Walsh, Mike (1991). Productivity Sand Traps & Tar Pits: How to Detect and Avoid Them. New York: Dorset House Publishing.

Walsh, Myles E. (1981). Understanding Computers: What Managers and Users Need to Know. New York: John Wiley & Sons.

Walshe, T. J. (1933). Quest of Reality. Saint Louis, MO: B. Herder Book Company.

Warfield, J. N. (1987a). Education in Generic Design. Bela Banathy (Ed.). Design Inquiry, pp. 185-196. San Francisco: International Systems Institute & International Society for General Systems Research.

Warshaw, Leon J. (1979). Managing Stress. Reading, MA: Addison-Wesley Publishing Company.

Watkins, J. W. N. (1953). Ideal Types and Historical Explanation, in H. Feigl & M. Brodbeck (EDs.), Readings in the Philosophy of Science. New York.

Watkins, J. W. N. (1958). The Alleged Inadequacy of Methodological Individualism, Journal of Philosophy, LV (1958).

Watkins, J. W. N. (1959). Historical Explanation in the Social Sciences, in Patrick Gardiner (Ed.), Theories of History. New York.

Watson, Paul K. (2005). Living Purpose: The Study of Purpose in the Living World as a Sources of New Spiritual Information, Spiritual Information 100 Perspectives on Science and Religion, Charles L. Harper, Jr. (Ed.). Philadelphia, PA: Templeton Foundation Press. (p. 301).

Weber, Zach: Paradox and Foundation. Submitted in Total Fulfillment of the Requirements of the Degree of Doctor of Philosophy. May 2009

Website: Official G.S. Altshuller Foundation. http://www.altshuller.ru. Last seen: 01.12.2013.

Website: Ideation International Inc. http://www.ideationtriz.com. Last seen: 01.12.2013.

Website: http://www.metodolog.ru Last seen: 01.12.2013.

Website: Wikipedia: TRIZ. http://en.wikipedia.org/wiki/TRIZ. Last seen: 01.12.2013.

Weinberg, Gerald M. (1975). An Introduction to General Systems Thinking. New York: John Wiley & Sons.

Weinberg, Gerald M. (1982). Overstructured Management of Software Engineering. Proceedings, Sixth International Conference of Software Engineering. Washington, D.C: IEEE Computer Society. Pp.2-8.

Weinberg, Gerald M. (1986). Becoming a Technical Leader: An Organic Problem-Solving Approach. New York: Dorset House Publishing Company.

Weinberg, Gerald M. (1992). Quality Software Management Volume 1 Systems Thinking. New York: Dorset House Publishing.

Weinberg, Harry L. (1959) Levels of Knowing and Existence. Harper & Brothers, Publishers New York.

Weisbord, Marvin R. (1987). Productive Workplaces: Organizing and Managing for Dignity, Meaning, and Community. San Francisco: Jossey-Bass Publishers

Weiss, Paul (1967). The Living System: Determinism Stratified, in Koestler & Smythies, Beyond Reductionism. New York.

Weiss, Paul (1967). One Plus One Does Not Equal Two, in G. C. Quarton, T. Melnechuk, & F. O. Schmitt (EDs.). The Neurosciences: A Study Program. New York.

Wexley & Yukl (1977). Organizational Behavior and Personnel Psychology. Homewood, IL: Richard D. Irwin, Inc.

Wheatley, Edward W. (1976). Values in Conflict. Miami: Banyan Books.

Wheelwright, Steven C. & Makridakis, Spyros (1980). Forecasting Methods for Management, 3rd Ed. New York: John Wiley & Sons.

Whitaker, Randall, Essler, Ulf & Ostberg, Olov (1991). Participatory Business Modeling. Sweden: Lulea University, Research Report, Tulea 1991: 31.

Whitehead, Alfred N. (1929). Process and Reality. New York: The Free Press.

Whyte, W.F. (ed.) (1991) Participatory Action Research. Sage: London.

Wilber, Ken (2000). Integral Psychology: Consciousness, Spirit, Psychology, Therapy. Shambhala Publications House, Boston, MA.

Wildman, Wesley J. (2005). Global Spiritual Confusion and the Neglected Problem of Excess Spiritual Information, Spiritual Information 100 Perspectives on Science and Religion, Charles L. Harper, Jr. (Ed.). Philadelphia, PA: Templeton Foundation Press. (pp. 33-38).

Williams, Raymond (1989). The Politics of Moderism. New York: Verso.

Wilson, Anne. Holistic Spirituality, Spirituality Today, Autumn 1988, Vol. 40 No. 3, pp. 208-219.

Wiseman, James A. Teaching Spiritual Theology: Methodological Reflections, Spirituality Today, Summer 1989, Vol. 41 No. 2, pp. 143-159.

Wittgenstein, L. (1961). Tractatus Logico-Philosophicus. London: Routledge & Kegan Paul.

Wolman, Benjamin D. (Ed.). (1973). Handbook of General Psychology. Englewood Cliffs: Prentice-Hall, Inc.

Wood, C. C., et al. (1987). Computer Security: A Comprehensive Controls Checklist. New York: John Wiley & Sons.

Woodcock, Alexander & Davis, Monte (1978). Catastrophe Theory. New York: Penguin.

Woodson, Wesley E. (1987). Human Factors Reference Guide for Electronics and Computer Professionals. New York: McGraw-Hill Book Company.

Wooldridge, Susan, Corder, Colin, & Johnson, Calude (1973). Security Standards for Data Processing. New York: John Wiley $ Sons.

Wriston, Walter B. (1992). The Twilight of Sovereignty: How the Information Revolution is Transforming Our World. New York: Charles Scribner's Son's.

Yolles M. I. (1996): Critical Systems Thinking, Paradigms, and the Modelling Space. Systems Practice,

Yourdon, Edward (1975). Case Studies in Object Oriented Analysis and Design, Yourdon Press.

Yourdon, Edward (1975). Structured Design. Yourdon Press.

Yourdon, Edward (1989). Modern Structured Analysis. Englewood Cliffs, Yourdon Press.

Yourdon, Edward (1992). Decline & Fall of the American Programmer. Englewood Cliffs: Yourdon Press.

Yourdon, Edward (1994). Object Oriented Systems Design. Yourdon Press.

Yourdon, Edward, (1996). Rise and Resurrection of the American Programmer, Prentice Hall.

Yourdon, Edward (2002). Managing High Intensity Internet Projects, Yourdon Press.

Zandar, Alvin (1994). Making Groups Effective, 2nd Edition. Jossey Bass Publishers, San Francisco.

Zedeck, Sheldon & Mosier, Kethleen (1990, February). Work in the Family and Employing Organization, American Psychologist. 45(2), pp. 24-251.

Zerzan, John & Carnes, Alice (1988). Questioning Technology. London: Freedom Press.

Zlotin B. & Litvin S. (1977). Creative Imagination Development, St. Petersburg, 1977 (in Russian: Злотин Б., Литвин С. Развитие Творческого Воображения. Ленинград, 1977)

Zlotin B., Zusman A., Altshuller G. & Philatov V. (1999). Tools of Classical TRIZ, Ideation International, 1999

Zlotin B. and Zusman A. (2001). Directed Evolution: Philosophy, Theory and Practice, Ideation International Inc., 2001

Zuboff, Shoshana (1984). In the Age of the Smart Machine: The Future of Work and Power. New York: Basic Books.

Zuker, Elaina (1991). The Seven Secrets of Influence. New York: McGraw-Hill, Inc.

Zvegintzov, N. (1982). What Life? What Cycle? Proceedings of the National Computer Conference. Reston, VA: AFIPS Press, pp. 563-568.

Zwart, Martin (1990). Constraint Driven Design/Engineering. Amsterdam: P.Q. Information Group, b.v., Mosselaan 57, 1934 PJ, Egmond a/d Hoef Netherlands.

Zwart, Martin (1991a). Integration of Workflow & EXTRA. Amsterdam: P.Q. Information Group, b. v.

Zwart, Martin (1991b). Object Documentation System. Amsterdam: P.Q. Information Group.

About the Author

Raymond L. Newkirk, Psy.D., Ph.D., Ph.D., Th.C., C.Q.A., F.B.I.M., I.O.M.

Founder, Entrepreneur, Product Architect, Inventive Problem Solver, Virtual-Learning Pioneer, Deep Technology Scientist, Thought Leader, Consultant, Mentor, Publisher Author, Speaker, Internationally Ranked Athlete

Raymond L. Newkirk is an internationally respected consulting specialist having earned advanced degrees and certifications in several disciplines including Ph.Ds. in the Philosophy of Science and Behavioral Science, Psy.D. in Clinical Psychology, Th.C., in Theology and the Ph.D. with Distinction in Human Science. Dr. Newkirk originated the Ulthule™ approach to human performance and the Applied Intuitive Solutions™ Inventive Problem- Solving Knowledge Base System. His professional background includes a distinguished career in multicultural research, human system design, and executive development. He has presented the Keynote Address to global audiences.

He is the Founder & CEO of the Systems Management Institute, a firm that applies human systems design to the building of high-performance organizations. He was Founder and Chairman of Bay University, an innovative E-Learning Company. He has enjoyed a life-long interest in business and enterprise incubation. He founded his first company at the age of 16, a janitorial service with three employees, and has organized start-ups & joint ventures ever since.

Dr. Newkirk has served in diverse industries and executive capacities. He was a Senior Fellow of the Monterey Bay Management Group. He served as Chief Operating Officer of Mindmaker, Inc. of San Jose, California, an early A/I and neural net pioneer that won Best of Comdex two years consecutively during the dot.com revolution in Silicon Valley. He also served as President and Chief Operating

Officer of P.Q. Information Group, b.v. the Netherlands, an innovative company that pioneered Business Rules processing software development, and Founder of the International Association of Information Management.

He led projects for the Minister of Defense and Aviation and the Royal Saudi Naval Forces for the Kingdom of Saudi Arabia and for the Office of the President, Republic of the Philippines. Dr. Newkirk has led industry-changing engagements for Southwest Bell, Bank of America, and Dell Computers. He was a VIP Priority Guest of the CNN World Business Development Congress. He was invited as a visiting Ambassador in Business Development and Technology Transfer to the Soviet Union and as an expert guest to development conferences in Cairo, Egypt and Oxford, England. He conducted seminars for Technology Transfer, Rome, I.B.C. London and Amsterdam and S.I.B.C. Jeddah, Kingdom of Saudi Arabia.

Dr. Newkirk never stops writing. A prolific writer, he has published more than 1,600 articles, monographs, books, e-learning courses, blogs, and guest columns for the San Francisco Examiner. His latest book, Navigating Sociopaths at Work, will be available early in 2020. His most recent book, Leading by Design, has become a widely sought collector's book that is available through the Systems Management Institute Press, Amazon, or Booklocker Press. His next book series, Ray Newkirk Tackles Workplace Relationships, advances a fresh look at leadership thinking and establishes the foundation for a new science of Leadership. He has authored works in English, Italian, Russian, Arabic, and Latin.

He is the producer of the Ray Newkirk Library Series. He advocates the intellectual, physical, and spiritual development of the person. He studied philosophy as a Benedictine Monk in Italy and studied theology with the Franciscan Friars in Washington D.C. He participated for many years with the Amateur Athletic Union (AAU) both as a competitor and supporter.

Early in his athletic career, he attained international ranking in Olympic Weightlifting having won 12 championships and set 22 competitive records in the sport. He won Outstanding Weightlifter Award, Ohio State A.A.U. A few of his many records still stand today. Currently, he is in training to compete in the Masters World Championships and was the reigning Pacific Weightlifting Association Masters Champion where he is still in the business of chasing records.

As an amateur explorer, Ray went diving in the Red Sea, mountain climbing in Alaska, worked as a deck hand on Dutch freighter, sailed in the Bahamas, and enjoyed deep-sea fishing in the Caribbean, among other global adventures.

Dr. Newkirk is an innovative social thinker. He is concerned about the problems facing the elderly in this technological and fast paced age. He has conducted workshops for senior citizens & executives on health, nutrition, and stress management. He established a health clinic and medical network for the elderly. He also contributed to the establishment of an orphanage in the Third World, funded fellowships for students in Eastern Europe to travel abroad and participate in seminars and professional training, and established a Southeast Asian International Fellowship. Dr. Newkirk's Guiding Perspective is:

Life, Love, Leadership, Growth, & Honor
"Live life fully. Love deeply with wisdom.
Lead others to great achievement.
Grow spiritually and intellectually.
Honor God in all I do."

Visit www.drraynewkirk.com
or
email: rnewkirk@smilc.info

SMI

Systems Management Institute

Don't miss out!

Visit the website below and you can sign up to receive emails whenever Raymond Newkirk, Psy.D., Ph.D., Ph.D. publishes a new book. There's no charge and no obligation.

https://books2read.com/r/B-A-ASCN-ZGHLB

BOOKS 2 READ

Connecting independent readers to independent writers.

Did you love *Insider Threat Prevention*? Then you should read *Adventures in Paleo Leadership*[1] by Raymond Newkirk, Psy.D., Ph.D., Ph.D.!

[2]

Leadership is a vital topic in every profession from. Business, Education, Government. and Defense to Religion, Science, Medicine, and Law Enforcement, and on and on and on. Leadership often makes the difference between success and failure. It is one of those topics that fuels the emotions of just about everyone from age ten to one hundred. Everyone seems to have an opinion about Leadership. These opinions frequently contradict one another as they generate confusion among followers. I wrote "Adventures in Paleo Leadership" to take us back, way way back, to that time when Leadership first began to emerge in recorded human affairs and follow its evolutionary unfolding to

1. https://books2read.com/u/mekZal

2. https://books2read.com/u/mekZal

better understand what Leadership is and how it became so confusing and complicated as it has become over the last several decades. From Mysticism to Psychology and all topics in between, Leadership has been part to the human landscape since human beings first started being together. ---- Raymond L. Newkirk

Also by Raymond Newkirk, Psy.D., Ph.D., Ph.D.

Cosmic Truth God, Us and Them
Cosmic Truth God, Us, and Them

Executive Life in the 21st Century
Executive Life in the 21st Century Part One: Leadership in the Age of Cyber Terror

Love All Around
Love All Around

Paleo-Leadership
Adventures in Paleo Leadership
Reconstructed Leadership

The Psychology of Insider Threat Prevention

Part Two: Unifying Continuous Performance Management and
Insider Threat Prevention Cyber Security
Insider Threat Prevention
Psychology of Insider Threat Prevention Part 4

Standalone
Dr. Raymond Leslie Newkirk On Who We Are
Time to Get Serious
Psychopaths at Work